Vigilante Newspapers

VIGILA
NEWS

A TALE OF SEX, RELIGION, AND

UNIVERSITY OF WASHINGTON PRESS *Seattle and London*

NTE PAPERS

MURDER IN THE NORTHWEST

GERALD J. BALDASTY

This book is published in memory of Marsha L. Landolt (1948–2004),
Dean of the Graduate School and Vice Provost, University of Washington,
with the support of the University of Washington Press Endowment.

UNIVERSITY OF WASHINGTON PRESS
PO Box 50096, Seattle, WA 98145
www.washington.edu/uwpress

LIBRARY OF CONGRESS CATALOGING-IN-PUBLICATION DATA
Baldasty, Gerald J.
Vigilante newspapers : a tale of sex, religion, and murder in the Northwest /
Gerald J. Baldasty.
p. cm.
Includes bibliographical references and index.
ISBN 0-295-98529-1 (pbk. : alk. paper)
1. Creffield, Edmund, 1867?-1906. 2. Mitchell, George (George Washington),
1883?-1906. 3. Church of the Bride of Christ. 4. Newspapers—Objectivity.
5. Religion and the press—Oregon. I. Title.
BP605.C546B35 2005   979.5'34—dc22   2005016363

The paper used in this publication is acid-free and 90 percent recycled from at least 50
percent post-consumer waste. It meets the minimum requirements of American National
Standard for Information Sciences—Permanence of Paper for Printed Library Materials,
ANSI Z39.48–1984. ♾ ♻

Cover (left to right): detail photo of George Mitchell from *Seattle Star,* 7 May 1906;
detail photo of Esther Mitchell from *Seattle Star,* 13 July 1906; detail photo of Edmund
Creffield courtesy of Oregon State Archives, Penitentiary Records, Case File 4941

Contents

Acknowledgments

I AM INDEBTED to many for their assistance during this project. The University of Washington provided a sabbatical leave from teaching, and the School of Communications and its director, C. Anthony Giffard, provided a grant from the William K. Test Trust.

I wrote much of this manuscript as a visiting scholar at Indiana University's Institute for Advanced Study. My thanks to Mary Ellen Brown, director, and Ivona Hedin, assistant director. My thanks as well to other colleagues who have provided thoughtful and useful advice, including Ray Hedin, Indiana University, and John Nerone, University of Illinois.

Space and imperfect memory preclude thanking everyone who helped me over the years. To mention a few: I am indebted to my colleagues in the School of Communications and its successor Department of Communication for creating an intellectual community that values research. My thanks, in particular, to those who helped nurture this project with their interest and comments: Lance Bennett, David Domke, Richard Kielbowicz, Valerie Manusov, Patricia Moy, Don Pember, Nancy Rivenburgh, and Roger Simpson. Other colleagues at the University of Washington have been very supportive, too, and in particular I thank Susan Jeffords and Judy Howard. My department staff has provided assistance in many ways—my thanks to Nancy Dosmann, Patricia Humphrey, Victoria Sprang and Eunice Yang.

I have benefited enormously from the support of many in the UW Libraries. My thanks to Cindy Blanding and Barbara Grayson of Interlibrary Loan; Glenda Pearson and Terry Kato of Microforms-Newspapers; Jessica Albano of Reference; and Carla Rickerson of Special Collections. Thanks, also, to Richard Engeman of the Oregon Historical Society; to Martin Burgess at the Seattle Public Library; to Nancy Hines at the University of Washington Classroom Support Services; and to Will Blethen and Pat Foote at the *Seattle Times*.

My students and research assistants have, as always, been a particular inspiration in thinking about research and the broader social role of the media. Thanks to April Peterson, Robert Newell, Pattijean Hooper, Mark LaPointe, Verena Hess, and particularly Meredith Li Vollmer and Meg Spratt for their wonderful ideas and help.

I greatly appreciate the enthusiasm and insight provided by the staff of the University of Washington Press; my thanks to Pat Soden, Naomi Pascal, Marilyn Trueblood, and Lita Tarver. Michael Duckworth has been a steady critic and advocate, and thus an ideal editor.

Family and friends helped, too—far more than they realize. Thanks to Richard Baldasty, Trudy Tatham, Anna Baldasty, Helena Baldasty, Deborah DeWolfe, Kate Stewart, Tom Greer, Dennis King, and Jan Ames. Most of all, my thanks to Randy Beam for his thoughtful criticism and enduring support.

Vigilante Newspapers

Introduction

NEARLY A DECADE AGO, while working on a research project on the history of press competition, I came across newspaper accounts of a murder trial in Seattle in 1906. One of the risks in reading old newspapers is the temptation to get sidetracked by interesting or odd stories, and I soon found myself reading about George Mitchell's trial for the murder of Edmund Creffield.

Based on a cursory reading of the Mitchell story, I guessed—correctly, it turned out—that Mitchell would go free even though he admitted to tracking down and killing Creffield. What really sparked my curiosity, however, was the fact that I came away from my newspaper reading with the sense that an acquittal was the *right* verdict, and that George Mitchell really was a hero. What were the cues—in language, emphasis, or advocacy—that led to that conclusion? It seemed clear that something beyond a simple report of the facts was being presented.

A brief review of the articles about George Mitchell revealed several characteristics of the coverage and raised more questions. First, the George Mitchell case was a major story, characterized by large headlines and vivid prose. Turn-of-the-century urban newspapers often presented the news in an agitated fashion that served to magnify the drama of events. What was it about this story that merited that level of involvement? Why did it have such a particular hold on the interest of editors and reporters? Second, the Seattle press was clearly advocating on George Mitchell's behalf, running editorials and commentary that ardently defended him. This sympathy of mainstream newspapers for a confessed murderer seemed odd. The U.S. media have usually kept fairly close ties to the establishment, and as such, have been strong defenders of law and order. What brought the press to a position from which premeditated murder was somehow defensible or even admirable? Third, the "facts" of the case could easily have been the basis for reports that portrayed George Mitchell as a premeditating murderer who snuck up on his unarmed victim and gunned him down in cold blood. What generated the positive portrait of George Mitchell instead, and why did it seem so plausible?

The larger issue here is the tremendous power of the press—as an advocate, teacher, and interpreter of the day's events. U.S. newspapers long have offered strong opinions on the issues of the day, and long have influenced public policy and individual beliefs. Early-nineteenth-century newspapers were saturated with ardent political advocacy; that advocacy was their reason for existence. Even with the rise of a more market-oriented (and consequently less partisan) press since the 1880s, editorials have continued to provide national and local leadership on a wide variety of issues. In George Mitchell's case, Seattle newspapers churned out editorials and commentary that helped make him a hero and win an acquittal.

Beyond that overt advocacy, the Seattle press was influential because of the way it defined the news about George Mitchell. This task of news definition speaks to two important processes: the selection of "facts" and sources (what to include or exclude; whom to interview), and the broader interpretation of the news. In the Mitchell case, the press consistently presented facts and relied on sources that were sympathetic to Mitchell, while generally ignoring other facts or sources. That alone guaranteed a particularly positive profile of Mitchell. In addition, through both their own commentary and that of sources, the newspapers defined what was good or bad, what was admirable or despicable, what was appropriate or inappropriate. By repeatedly linking George Mitchell to highly prized social values such as family devotion, responsibility, bravery, and the need for the strong to protect the weak, the press created a powerful and convincing portrait of him not as a criminal but as a hero. In a broader arena, by presenting these values as natural and good, the press also reinforced them and the social roles implicit in them. The press was thus both a reporter and a teacher—about George Mitchell and about a broader array of values. The wide reach of the press makes it a powerful force in defining and reinforcing social values.

Of course the press is not a completely independent agent, and this advocacy and news definition took place within a larger political, social, and economic context. For much of the nineteenth century, individual newspapers served as the organ of a particular political party, and that alliance clearly determined the nature of their advocacy. In the late nineteenth and early twentieth centuries, as newspapers distanced themselves from political parties, they increasingly competed with each other for circulation among readers of any and all parties. Competition influenced the definition of news, particularly as newspapers sought to differentiate themselves in the marketplace by appealing to different audience segments (such as the working class) or by stressing organizational expertise (e.g., getting the news before others). All of this was to play a role in defining the news about George Mitchell and his victim.

Not all events or issues become fodder for press advocacy or for broader discourses on social values. In the early 1900s, the case of George Mitchell and the man he killed, Edmund Creffield, presented an ideal situation—a "perfect storm," if you will—for press advocacy, news definition, and larger lessons on social issues. The case dealt with a host of issues—religion, sex, gender roles, family values, insanity, morals—that drew sharp reactions from many. The nascent Pentecostal movement was challenging traditional modes of worship and belief, while "modern" notions of women's rights and roles in society challenged traditional gender norms and—at least in the eyes of some—undermined the institution of family. The social issues surrounding the Mitchell-Creffield case were ones of particular moment in the country at large, and thus all the more likely to generate press attention and moralizing.

The Press in the Early 1900s

In the early 1900s, the press was in a period of transition in U.S. society, becoming a truly mass medium and, in the process, taking on a larger and more significant social role than ever before. This was particularly true in urban areas, where the sheer size and scope of activity meant that many people experienced the world increasingly through the media rather than through firsthand observation.

The press had long played a prominent role in American political life. Partisan papers began to flourish soon after independence, and by the Jacksonian era, much of political life and organization was centered on partisan newspapers and their editors. By the late nineteenth century, however, the press had moved away from that fairly narrow focus to become purveyors of information on a wide variety of topics—including sports, society and fashion, theater, literature, crime, accidents, and business—that invariably drew more readers and that also involved the press increasingly in issues dealing with the everyday lives of readers. Columnists offered advice on marriage, family life, raising children, and managing the home. Short stories focused on adventure, but also on love, marriage, and disappointment. Editorials spoke not just of politics but of broader political-social issues, such as poverty and divorce.

Driven both by customer interest and by economic factors, the press grew dramatically. Between 1880 and 1904, the number of daily newspapers published in the United States more than doubled, rising from 971 to 2,452; the number of weekly newspapers almost doubled, rising from 8,633 to 15,046. The circulation of daily newspapers rose from 3.5 million in 1880 to 19.6 million in 1904.[1]

Extensive circulation and diversified content gave the press a position of particular influence, and journalists and social commentators recognized this power. One prominent editor argued that the press's power stemmed from the way it framed the news: "It takes men when their information is incomplete, when their reasoning has not yet been worked out, when their opinions have not yet been fixed, and it suggests and intimates and insinuates an opinion and a judgment which oftentimes a man . . . adopts as something established and concluded."[2] A Portland, Oregon, minister noted that "the editor is a preacher whose pulpit reaches around the globe." He noted that the wide reach of the newspaper made it an extremely powerful social institution with real influence in the everyday lives of readers:

> We find it upon the breakfast table, in the dining room, the office, the shop, wherever man goes the paper goes. It is the only library multitudes ever think of or care for. All there is for them of art, culture, history and literature flows in to their lives through the columns of the daily newspaper. Men who never enter a church read its religious intelligence; who never open a volume of history, read its editorials . . . maiden and youth linger over its stories and borrow their early dreams from its columns.[3]

A sociologist at the University of Chicago at the turn of the century wrote that the press had great power, noting that "language is a powerful instrument of control because through it, knowledge, tradition, standpoint, ideals, stimulations are transmitted and increased." Another critic argued that the press had a vast influence on beliefs and behavior, contending that articles detailing suicides caused other suicides.[4]

Competition was intense, as newspapers vied with one another for circulation and revenues. Large cities had many competing newspapers. In 1899, New York City had twenty-nine daily and Sunday newspapers.[5] In 1905, Seattle had four daily newspapers, as did Portland, Oregon. Newspapers jockeyed with each other to get the news first. In an era when most newspapers sales were on the street (rather than through home-delivery subscriptions), a scoop might mean hundreds or thousands of additional sales, or even a revenue-boosting "extra" edition. Newspapers also competed with one another by adopting quasi-populist stances to win public favor—crusades for cheap prices on ice in summer or coal in winter were common. Advocacy was not gone, but the traditional focus on party politics of the early nineteenth century was now replaced by a focus on the everyday lives of readers.

There was, at times, a good deal of recklessness as newspapers vied for readers. Reporters sometimes fabricated stories, to guarantee that they had a story that no other reporter had. The mania for scoops also led to errors: one newspaper's extra edition anticipated the death of President McKinley by several hours. The sensational "yellow" journalism of late-1890s New York City was replete with fabrication, innuendo, and half-truth. William Randolph Hearst's highly exaggerated and biased coverage of Spanish rule in Cuba was condemned by many, but it flourished in an occupational culture devoid of broad ethical norms. Journalism historian Ted Curtis Smythe notes that "newsgathering ethics were ad hoc . . . on most papers, inexperienced reporters and editors learned on the job, and the dominant theme was to write stories that attracted the attention of editors, who believed stories sold newspapers." There were a few thoughtful press critics and commentators in that era, but the fledgling mass press of the early 1900s was engaged in a highly competitive game for which there were few rules.[6]

Outside urban areas, newspapers also played a growing role in social life. In small-town America, the older format of ardent partisanship still flourished. Newspapers still readily identified with a specific party (Republican, Democrat, Populist, etc.) and served as organs for those parties. But even these small-town newspapers were changing, and like their big-city counterparts they became increasingly attentive to the everyday lives of their readers. They also diversified their key economic alliances; although still close to political parties, they were also very much tied to local business interests that provided increasingly important advertising revenue.

Newspapers in the Pacific Northwest reflected these national trends. The larger metropolitan dailies, in Portland and Seattle, offered readers a wide array of content, ranging from traditional political news to coverage of leisure activities (such as sports and theater), so-called women's news (society, fashion, cooking), and news about business, accidents, fires, court cases, and religion. The moral transgressions of rich and poor alike were fair game for the press. Seattle newspapers told of love triangles, adultery, and acrimonious divorce cases. They ran columns on courtship, marriage, and family life. The unusual always drew attention: midgets who married, old men who married very young women, poor orphans who became successful.

Competition for readers was often intense in Portland and Seattle. In Seattle, the *Seattle Times* and the *Star*—both daily afternoon newspapers, both owned by strong-willed men with healthy egos—battled

hard for primacy in circulation. They both hit upon a series of strat-
agems to boost circulation, holding contests, sponsoring parades,
and advocating a host of popular measures such as cheap electricity,
improved public transportation, and public safety. Both the *Times* and
the *Star* promoted themselves grandiosely, touting claims of scoops,
superb printing quality, and thorough news coverage. One biogra-
phy nicely captured the character of Alden J. Blethen, the publisher
of the *Times*: "Vital, stubborn, pugnacious, he was a man of ordinary
gifts who pursued greatness, a reformer plagued by vices, a relentless
enemy and an indulgent friend." Edward W. Scripps, the owner of
the *Star*, was a skillful business strategist who combined high-minded
advocacy for working-class interests with a blaring brass-band style of
self-promotion, vivid headlines, and frenzied crusades. "A good newspaper is one that will sell," he maintained.[7] The competition between
Blethen and Scripps did much to define journalism in Seattle.

In smaller towns, such as Corvallis, Oregon, newspapers continued
to wear their party affiliations openly, but partisan advocacy was pronounced primarily at election time. During the rest of the year, these
weekly (or twice-weekly) newspapers increasingly diversified to cover
local business, schools, churches, and social associations. As party
patronage gave way to advertising as the chief source of newspaper
revenue, small-town newspapers joined their big-city counterparts
in providing generous support for local businesses. In this role as
civic boosters, small-town newspapers showcased the good about their
towns, hoping to lure new settlers and improve business. In the local
elites that dominated public and even private life in these small towns,
editors were close partners with politicians and businesspeople.

The Social Role of Women in the Early 1900s

Just as the press was in transition in the early 1900s, so too were the
definitions of women's social roles and responsibilities. On the one
hand, traditionalists insisted that a woman's place was in the home—
as wife, mother, and nurturer. President Theodore Roosevelt's well-
publicized warning against "race suicide" exhorted women to recognize their obligation to be "a good wife, a good mother, able and
wiling to perform the first and greatest duty of womanhood, healthy

children, sound in body, mind and character, and numerous enough so that the race increase and not decrease." Roosevelt was hardly alone in his view. Advice manuals, a highly popular form of media culture in the nineteenth and early twentieth centuries, reinforced the notion of woman as the center of the home. Mary Virginia Terhune, the author of a dozen advice books in the latter decades of the nineteenth century under the pseudonym Marion Harland, reminded women that their true calling was to serve family and nation through the home. Although some women argued for a broader mission in society, Harland cautioned that there was no higher mission than the "heaven appointed task" of homemaker and mother. Harland compared women's work to that of the "chink filler" who did the final and crucial work of building a home by filling in the cracks around logs or windows:

> It requires vast patience and much love for one's fellow man to be a chink filler. She it is who, as wife, mother, sister, or perhaps, maiden-aunt, picks up the hat or gloves Mamie has carelessly left on the drawing-room table, wipes the tiny finger smears from the window panes at which baby stood to wave his hand to pap this morning, dusts the rungs of the chair neglected by the parlor maid and mends the ripped coat which Johnny forgot to mention until it was nearly time to start for school.[8]

In everyday life, however, women were challenging the views that strictly confined them to home and motherhood. Birth rates were slowly declining, and women were starting to take jobs outside the home. Social-reform causes drew women to a variety of public associations, such as the Young Women's Christian Association. Even though by 1900 suffragists were still often couching their advocacy for voting rights in terms of motherhood (i.e., the need to educate their children to be citizens required mothers to be full citizens) rather than natural rights, they were boldly claiming a place in the public sphere long monopolized by men. Media referred to "the new woman": an educated, ambitious, and socially active creature who refused to be defined solely in terms of responsibilities to husband and children.[9]

All of this meant that many Americans, including journalists, were particularly attentive to the topic of women's roles and responsibilities. The issue was being agitated in American life and society; as historian Jean Matthews notes, the "public encomiums to 'home' and woman's role within it grew louder as more women showed an inclination to escape its hold." Women's magazines, such as *Ladies Home Journal* and *Good Housekeeping*, presented women as happy and healthy when they focused on home and family, and general-interest magazines echoed this view. Writing in the general-interest magazine *The Independent* in 1901 that womanly women stay at home, Henry Finck contended that "The invasion of man's domain by women is not a matter of social evolution and progress, but a temporary anomaly against which a strong reaction has already set in." Suffrage, he continued, would "inflict a grievous wrong on the vast majority of women—the womanly women—as well as on children, on men and society in general." *Atlantic Monthly* offered: "If man attempts woman's function, he will prove himself but an inferior woman. If woman attempts man's function she will prove herself but an inferior man. Some masculine women there are . . . these are the monstrosities of nature."[10]

The Mitchell case didn't deal with "the new woman," suffrage, or even women's roles outside the home. But it did focus on gender-defined family loyalties and obligations; as such, it easily was subsumed in the broader social discourse about women and society.

A Sensational Story

The story of George Mitchell first drew the attention of the Seattle press because it was so dramatic. How many murderers readily and calmly admit their guilt, as did Mitchell? The story remained prominent—with more than 200 articles in the *Times* and the *Star* in the summer of 1906—because it lent itself to a vivid reporting style: a self-styled hero who redeems his sister's honor by killing a demonic cult leader. It was a story with heroes and villains, human pathos and tattered lives—in other words, a story very likely to garner a good deal of attention from the reading public. It was also a big story, the proverbial tip of the iceberg, the culmination of three years of religious frenzy, controversy, and scandal.

The story had started in 1903, when a band of zealots inspired by a charismatic, eccentric leader, Edmund Creffield, developed bizarre, sometimes sexualized religious practices that scandalized and enraged many in the community. Although its adherents were few, "Creffield-ism" engulfed the small town of Corvallis, Oregon, sundering families, arousing mobs, driving more than a dozen people to a state asylum, and eventually leading to two suicides and two murders, beginning with that of Creffield himself.

George Mitchell was drawn into this controversy because two of his sisters—Donna and Esther—came under Creffield's influence. In an era when men took quite seriously their role as protectors of women, Creffield's great power over these and other women invited retribution, and George Mitchell was just one of a dozen or more men who wanted to kill Edmund Creffield. Unlike the others, though, he succeeded.

Creffield was a polarizing figure—his followers worshipped him, while many skeptics thought him a demonic figure. Advocating a sim-ple, non-worldly life, Creffield induced his followers to burn their pos-sessions, wear minimal amounts of clothing, and eat only sparingly. Huge bonfires they lit in October 1903—with furniture, rugs, dishes, and purportedly even household pets consigned to the flames—seemed both a religious and a safety menace to many Corvallisites. Secret rituals caused scandal: tales circulated of sessions in which the "prophet" and his mostly female devotees, clad only in very light and loose-fitting clothes, rolled for hours together on the floor in what they claimed was religious ecstasy.

Creffield's followers came to see him as a great prophet, then as Christ. They likened his earthly travails, including a prison term in 1904 and 1905, to the persecution of Jesus. After his death, some of the flock expected him to rise from the grave. Others thought him anything but messianic: Corvallisites tarred and feathered him in early 1904, and newspapers vilified him, calling him a fanatic and worse. Many rejoiced when he was gunned down by George Mitchell.

What earned the Creffieldites the enmity of so many was the simple fact that they defied many of the social norms of the day. Their anti-materialistic tenets and their religious fervor seemed a far cry from conventional piety, and many devout Christians in Corvallis had dif-ficulty believing that rolling on the floor and shouting for hours at a time bore any resemblance to real religion. Although Creffield was no advocate of modern notions of women's rights, his teachings in effect challenged traditional gender roles, as his women followers deserted family and hearth in their zeal for constant worship. Moral scandal and outrage arose, too, as people discovered that Creffield had encouraged at least one woman to have sex with him as a way of "purifying" herself. Beyond this, Creffield became a pariah because he acutely embarrassed Corvallis' civic leaders. His notoriety threatened their ambitions for the town's growth and economic development, as Corvallis became known not as a wonderful place for new settlers but instead as a center of odd cult practices.

The press gave the story extensive coverage, with vivid headlines and startling detail. Newspapers in the Pacific Northwest, and particularly in Seattle and Corvallis, deeply influenced how both Creffield and Mitchell were seen by the public. The press also framed the news to provide not just an account of the saga of Edmund Creffield and George Mitchell but also a broader lesson about social values. It is this combination—defender of George Mitchell, social conscience—that makes the role of the press in this story so interesting and important.

The Mitchell-Creffield story indicates much about social issues and the press as an institution driving public opinion and beliefs, but this is also a story about individual lives. Although many were swept up in the potent mix of religion, sex, and vengeance that Creffield inspired, the most tragic story in this larger drama is that of two young siblings, Esther and George Mitchell. They were like characters in a Greek tragedy, each blinded by a singular vision that drove their reasoning and actions and led them to destroy one another. George was a prisoner of the traditional belief that a man must avenge a woman's dishonor. Armed with this certitude, he tracked down and killed Creffield to stop the practices he believed had "ruined" his sister and several other young women. Esther, in contrast, felt no need for protection from her brother. She had developed a strong loyalty to Creffield, and even after his death she remained his disciple and sought to avenge his death by murdering her own brother. But even then the tragedy was not over; despite treatment in a state asylum, Esther eventually killed herself.

It was always easy and often quite reasonable to blame Creffield for the tragedy that befell him and those around him. But the Creffield drama is not just a story about a small band of true believers whose enthusiasm led them astray. It is a larger story about the crosscurrents of American life in the early 1900s, including the power of the press as a social and moral arbiter, and society's reluctance to tolerate unconventional views about gender, family, and religion. Edmund Creffield and his followers challenged the conventions of behavior and morality of that era; for that, they paid a high price.

1 Collision Course

Corvallis' best days are yet to come, and the summit of her prosperity has been far from reached. Naught but words of confidence and enthusiasm are heard on every hand.

—CORVALLIS *TIMES*, JUNE 27, 1903

IN THE SUMMER OF 1903, Corvallis, Oregon, was a small and growing town of about 1,800, best known for its agricultural college and as the commercial center of a thriving agricultural area. Civic leaders were proud of their town's traditional values of hard work, family, and church. But they wanted much more. Eager for population growth and economic development, they were doing all they could in the early 1900s to lure new settlers and businesses to town. The Corvallis Citizens' League, made up of local businessmen, promoted immigration to the town by circulating pamphlets throughout the East and Midwest extolling the town's virtues. The Corvallis Improvement Society organized city beautification projects, such as the planting of trees and flowers, to impress potential settlers. One of the town's two newspapers, the *Times*, advocated starting an exhibit of local agricultural products at Portland's main train station, contending that "the sight of an unusually fine sheaf of wheat, a bunch of grass of exceptional length, or any other product of unusual merit appeals to a homeseeker with far greater directness and power than do pages and pages of literature." When the *Times*, early that summer, proclaimed that "Corvallis' best days are yet to come," it was invoking the optimism and ambition that drove much of the town's activity.

During that same summer, a relative newcomer in the community,

Edmund Creffield, was demonstrating another kind of ambition as he sought to save souls through a new religious practice. Creffield's goals were very different from those of Corvallis's civic leaders; indeed, if one thing was true, it was that Creffield held in contempt those who sought material gain. He urged his followers to renounce worldly goods and comforts, instructing them to dress plainly, eat sparingly, and live as simply as was humanly possible. Creffield's great vision was the re-creation of the Garden of Eden, where men and women could praise God all day without worry of food or shelter.

In the normal course of events, one would have expected Creffield to create little stir in Corvallis. He had only a small handful of followers, about twenty-five at most, and they didn't want to have any contact at all with the vast majority of Corvallisites, whom they called nonbelievers. So it is unlikely that anyone, in that summer of 1903, could have envisioned that Creffield and the ambitious little town were heading for a collision. But they were, as Creffield persisted in his efforts to re-create Eden on the banks of the Willamette River, and as Corvallisites became convinced that this self-styled religious leader was a danger to traditional values and threatened to derail the town's ambitious plans for growth and prosperity.

The Rise of Corvallis

Established in the mid-1840s at the junction of the Mary and Willamette rivers, Corvallis enjoyed the varied fortunes so common to many Western frontier towns.[1] Trade grew fitfully and fires regularly leveled wood-frame buildings. The town briefly served as territorial capital in the 1850s, but it quickly lost that prize to Salem. Early settlers from the Midwest and East supported themselves primarily through farming. They brought with them many of the traditional organizations of the society they had left behind, building churches and establishing social clubs and lodges, such as the Oddfellows and Masons, as well as two temperance organizations. Oregon Agricultural College, established in 1868, contributed greatly to the town's local importance. Corvallis residents recognized the college's economic potential and supported it through the donation of land and the construction of an administration building.

The first sustained commercial expansion came only after the arrival of the railroad in 1880. The town witnessed a small but relatively important building boom in the 1880s, with an increase in businesses, homes, and public buildings such as the courthouse, the city hall, and a new public school. The Benton County Board of Immigration, established in 1885, publicized the county to attract settlers from the Midwest, and this spurred population growth until the financial crisis of the Panic of 1893. The Panic slowed trade, bankrupted railroads, and temporarily halted Corvallis's expansion.

By the early 1900s, however, the economy had recovered. Although the town had grown by only 19 percent in the 1890s, its growth rate reached 150 percent in the first decade of the new century. On June 27, 1903, the Corvallis *Times* accurately proclaimed that the town had rebounded:

CORVALLIS

A MOST CHARMINGLY LOCATED PROSPEROUS CITY

*Keeping Step to the Music of Progress—Sketches of her
Leading Industries and Mercantile Establishments*

The *Times* article first described the town's many advantages, noting its excellent railroad service, which allowed it to serve as "the distributing point for a rich agricultural district." The paper noted the presence of Oregon Agricultural College and numerous businesses, all of which contributed to town's "steady growth and solid development." Then the paper provided short sketches of some two dozen local businesses, detailing the commercial success of local banks and of a wide variety of stores (furniture, bicycles, dry goods, confectioners, druggists, books) and services (hotels, laundries, foundries), while predicting even greater commercial expansion in the years ahead.[2]

With the economy improving in the early years of the new century, Corvallis's leaders vigorously redoubled their efforts to attract newcomers to the town. The belief was widespread that newcomers would work an economic miracle for Corvallis, increasing capital, benefiting current businesses, generating new businesses, and reducing taxes. There were challenges, of course: higher taxes were needed at first to pay for the schools, paved roads, and city water system that would attract newcomers, and nearby local towns were just as eager for growth. But all of that seemed manageable, and civic leaders were optimistic.[3]

Corvallis's civic leaders believed that their town would be particularly appealing to new settlers because of its traditional values of family, work, and religion. This was a town of farmers and small businesspeople, most living in simple but well-cared-for homes. Their lives were filled with the everyday events common to small towns across the country: church suppers, births, deaths, marriages, family visits, meetings of fraternal organizations, "at home" parties, recitals, and a wide variety of other activities. The typical local resident was a churchgoer who valued God, home, and family. These were hardworking, law-abiding, moral people, conscious of their responsibilities to family and community. As one Corvallis resident from that period, Minerva Kiger Reynolds, later recalled in her memoirs, "They also liked their neighbors. They visited back and forth and were always anxious to lend a helping hand to each other."[4]

Among those traditional values was a belief that a woman's proper role was as a homemaker who cooked and cleaned for husband and children. Minerva Reynolds later recalled that a woman's week was organized primarily by house-related work: Monday for washing, Tuesday for ironing, Wednesday for mending and darning, Friday for housecleaning, and Saturday for baking. Thursday was set aside for visits with friends and family, and Sunday was, of course, a day of worship and prayer.[5]

Corvallis's two newspapers recounted stories of local women who had a strong sense of family duty. They selflessly cared for ill children and aged parents, and one young woman even moved to another town to care for her ailing father. A few women worked outside the home, but those jobs usually were short-term endeavors that soon gave way to family obligations. The *Times* told of one local teacher who resigned her job to move to California to care for her brother's family because her sister-in-law was too ill to do the work herself. Family concerns belonged to men, too, who worked foremost as providers and, when needed, cared for sick wives or mothers. Family ties defined lives, chores, responsibilities, and even socializing, as dinners, trips, and vacations all served to unite family members who lived apart.[6]

Outside the home and family circle, most women in Corvallis busied themselves in traditional women's roles centering on church and women's groups such as the Methodist Women's Home Missionary Society, the Presbyterian Missionary Society, the Coffee Club, the Young Women's Christian Association, the Rebekah Lodge, and the Order of Eastern Star. Religious affiliation even helped to structure some of women's socializing, as various church groups combined religious work with entertainment. The *Times* reported on one such event on February 4, 1903:

> An afternoon tea was given Friday at the house of Mrs. Hays. . . . The affair was given by the ladies of the Christian church, and a feature was the presentation of a Bible to the guest of honor. The occasion was very pleasant. About twenty persons were present.

And, on June 7, 1903, on another:

> Wednesday afternoon was made very interesting for Congregationalists and their friends at the home of Mrs. E. B. Taylor. The guests numbered 65 and after a literary and musical programme, were daintily served with ices and punch.

On February 26, 1904, the *Gazette* reported on a tea held by the Presbyterian Women's Missionary Society: "a pleasant program of music, readings, etc., was followed by the usual lunch. About 40 of the good sisters testified to have a very enjoyable afternoon."

All of these activities created what the Corvallis *Times* in early summer 1903 called "one of the neatest, healthiest and most progressive little cities in the state of Oregon." The paper revealed the town's ambitions when it stated that commercial and industrial expansion were "limited only by the energy of our people in taking advantage of the opportunities that lie at our door." And it echoed the town's pride in traditional values when it praised the many "cozy cottages and handsome homes" and noted that "civic and fraternal organizations are well represented while many church organizations are in a flourishing condition."[7] This self-congratulatory air would soon vanish, however, as the town and its people faced the troubling rise of Edmund Creffield and his small band of followers.

The Rise of Edmund Creffield and "God's Anointed"

A rather short and slight man—standing about 5 feet, 6 inches, and weighing about 135 pounds—with a shock of washed-out blond hair, light blue eyes, a pale complexion, and a prominent forehead, Creffield was not a very imposing person physically.[8] Yet he possessed something far more compelling—an almost magnetic personality, what would later be described as a "hypnotic" power to draw people to him and his beliefs. Although he never attracted a very large following in town—his flock would number between twenty and twenty-five followers—his impact on the town was more dramatic and controversial than that of any other religious leader in its history. The notoriety that the town received because of Creffield was not what civic boosters had wanted.

The chief mystery of the Creffield case is Creffield himself. Who he was, where he came from, what he believed and taught, how he so mesmerized some of his followers—all of these remain somewhat vague. He himself did not grant interviews to reporters, and he taught his followers to shun not only the press but the world at large. To a great degree, he has been defined for history by those who opposed him.

Little is known about Creffield's life before he became such a divisive figure in Corvallis. Most likely, he was born in Germany, studied briefly for the priesthood, and then emigrated to the United States in the 1890s. His full name was Franz Edmund Creffield, although most newspaper articles at the height of his notoriety dropped the first name. How he got to Oregon is unclear; what is clear, however, is that he heard the Salvation Army's call to arms on the streets of Portland and enlisted in the Army's battle for souls. Always short of recruits and often dependent on drifters and poorly educated men to fill its ranks, the Salvation Army was greatly impressed with Creffield's intelligence and abilities, and probably asked few questions about his past or religious beliefs. His training was most likely limited, given the Army's shortage of personnel, but he advanced rapidly from private to captain. While in Portland, he taught classes and was a highly effective preacher at Army meetings and on the city's streets. Before long, he was sent to McMinnville, Grants Pass, and Corvallis.

Although Creffield did not stay in the Salvation Army for very long, he found there many of the beliefs and practices that would shape his own religious sect. In sharp contrast with most established religions of that era in the U.S., the Salvationists embraced a highly emotional practice characterized by sensational preaching and intense and often loud participation by the faithful. Army meetings could stretch on for hours, during which congregants would give testimony of their faith and sometimes shout, scream, or writhe on the floor. Salvationists sought to give members a distinct Army-based identity; they renounced worldly vanities such as fancy clothes, tobacco, alcohol, and other luxuries, and opted for a plain uniform and a life of self-denial. Marriage outside the Army was forbidden, and connections to non-Salvationist friends and family discouraged. As the historian Lillian Taiz writes, becoming a Salvation Army officer meant severing oneself from friends and family and adhering to a new community—the Army. Set apart from others by their distinctive uniform, reliance on military-style rank and command structure, fervent religiosity, and frequent rotation in field assignments, Salvationists turned to one another for spiritual and emotional strength as well as for company.[9]

The Salvationists took pride in the condemnation of others; indeed, Army founders William and Catherine Booth told their followers that opposition and persecution were proof that they were doing God's work. Established churches disliked the Army's sensational preaching, emotionalism, and opposition to the conventional methods of traditional religion. Liberal Protestant churches, particularly those accommodating modernist thinking on evolution or scriptural criticism, found little to like in the Army's literal interpretation of the Bible or in its millennialism, while more conservative clergymen warned that the Army's highly enthusiastic rituals endangered women's virtue. Some brewery owners hoped to derail the Army because of its virulent denunciation of alcohol, going so far as to hire mobs to attack Salvationists. Injuries were not uncommon; in the United States in the 1880s and 1890s, at least five Salvationists were killed in such attacks, and others suffered attempted lynchings and broken bones.

In Portland, a saloon owner turned a fire hose on Army members in 1886 when they took their brass band to his neighborhood. Such attacks only invigorated the Salvationists. As historian Roy Hattersley writes, "William Booth's special brand of hubris made him relish the bottles and the half-bricks which rained down on every open-air meeting. The devil only struck back when the devil took notice."[10]

Although Creffield's later teachings would incorporate the Army's amalgam of high emotionalism, social separatism, asceticism, and semi-masochism, he left the Army after just two years. The hierarchical nature of the Army was not to Creffield's liking, and as some of his colleagues from the Portland Salvation Army corps later recalled, he bridled at taking orders. His undisciplined theology also clashed with Army beliefs; although the Salvationists cultivated highly ecstatic religious meetings, they were quite conservative in their doctrine.[11]

Returning to Corvallis in late 1902, Creffield soon lured the core of local Salvationists to his own teaching—ultimately, even the local Salvation Army leader, Major Brooks, joined the Creffieldites. In Corvallis, about two dozen people had been affiliated with the Salvation Army. Among them was the family of Orlando V. (O. V.) Hurt, a respected Corvallis merchant and member of the Republican state central committee. Hurt's family—his wife, Sarah, daughters Maud and Mae, and son Frank—took quickly to the charismatic Creffield, as did many of the other Corvallis Salvationists, including members of the Starr, Hartley, and Mitchell families.

Young Esther Mitchell, just fifteen years old, became one of Creffield's most ardent disciples. Creffield's charisma and self-assurance were particularly appealing to this lonely and shy girl for whom life seemed to hold little. Born the youngest of seven children to a poor family in Newberg, Oregon, Esther was, for all practical purposes, orphaned at the age of six when her mother died and her father, Charles Mitchell, sent her to live with another local family. Esther's older siblings went to work, supporting themselves, while the two youngest brothers—George and Perry—remained at home with their father. Esther saw few of them regularly, although George felt a particular responsibility for her, and she retained close ties to just one sister, Donna (also known as Belle). Except for George and Perry, none of the family saw much of their father, who had always been overly strict and emotionally distant from his children. After his wife's death, Charles Mitchell became heavily involved in the Salvation Army. O. V. Hurt later recalled that Mitchell often ignored his family in order to attend Army meetings: "Everything had to yield to his religious passion." Several of the older Mitchell children also joined the Salvation Army, and Esther eventually went to live in Corvallis with the Hurt family, also Army members.[12] Creffield's particular brand of religion was thus not entirely foreign to Esther, and he also offered her what her family had not: attention. It was a heady experience for a naïve young small-town girl.

A number of the young women attracted to Creffield came from broken families. Donna and Esther Mitchell had lost their mother and suffered from their father's indifference to them and obsession with religion. Rose, Florence, and Edna Seeley's father had deserted the three sisters after their mother died. Attie Bray suffered from a psychologically abusive father who repeatedly told her she was a sinner. Other followers, however, came from more comfortable and supportive homes. Another pair of sisters, Mollie and Olive Sandell, became part of the sect, as did Cora Hartley and her daughter, Sophie. A few men joined, too, although only Frank Hurt would remain a close member of the group in the following months and years. One Corvallis-area historian, Marlene McDonald, suggests that "everyone who became caught up with Creffield, especially the women, were lonely, needy, felt abandoned, or were left to themselves for long periods of time. . . . All these followers seemed to be looking for security, a sense of belonging, and perhaps freedom from the strictures of prim and proper Victorian society."[13]

Creffield and his followers were best known for their highly emotional and often frenzied services, which included shouting, praying, hymn singing, and rolling on the floor. At first, when they were meeting in town, the small band of believers began to alarm Corvallisites because the noisy services would go into the late hours—sometime as late as 2 or 3 A.M. Corvallis resident Minerva Kiger Reynolds, who was about ten at that time, later recalled those concerns:

They became the talk of the town. Some people were alarmed, others merely curious. But all were concerned. We lived about two blocks, in a direct line, from the meeting place and could hear them yelling and screaming, far into the night.

Reynolds recounted the experiences of curious Corvallisites, such as her mother, who dropped by the services:

> There was a low platform at the front of the room on which a woman was lying, covered with a sheet. Creffield was standing beside her, passing his hand back and forth above her and seemed to be praying that the Lord would take her up bodily to Heaven. Other women were either kneeling or sitting on the floor, their eyes closed as they pounded on benches with their fists, as they cried, "God have mercy," or "God will have victory tonight!"[14]

In the summer of 1903, the sect moved to an island in the Willamette River. There, far from town, they continued or perhaps even increased the fervor of their sessions. They kept the curious away, shunning those who were not part of their group. This seclusion naturally bred rumor, and accusations surfaced of scandalous behavior—including nudity—in the group.[15] An apostate follower later described the island activities as a mixture of shouting, rolling on the ground, Biblical literalism, and exorcism rituals—all conducted with an ecstatic frenzy. He claimed that, at one point, Creffield flogged a male follower with tree branches to drive the devil out of him.[16]

This frenzied style of worship caused the greatest concern in the early months of the sect's existence, but the substance of Creffield's teachings was also a source of concern to some in Corvallis. With a mixture of asceticism and hubris, Creffield proclaimed that he and his tiny sect had been called by God—"God's Anointed"—to create a new Eden, making way for the next coming of Christ. He exhorted his followers to abandon sinful worldly pleasures so as to concentrate all the more on God. Clothing, fancy food, material possessions, concern for appearance—all these were part of the sinful world that must be renounced. Minerva Reynolds later recalled Creffield's teachings:

> He disliked clothing, claiming it was "vile" and would tear off his garments. The women exchanged their clothes for "Mother

Creffield's Followers in Camp at Kiger's Island

Camp meeting group at Kiger's Island in 1903. From left to right; top row: Levins, Brooks, Julia Lamberson, Edna Seeley, Esther Mitchell, Wesley Seeley, Mrs. Frank Hurt (nee Sophia Hurt), Sophia Hartley, Ora Baldwin, Campbell. From left to right, bottom row: Mrs. Lewis Hartley, Mrs. Waldron (Portland), Mrs. Burt Starr, Mrs. Clarence Starr, Mae Hurt, Mrs. [Frank Hurt], Creffield, Mrs. Victor Hurt, Rose Seeley, Atta Bray.

*Creffield solidified his hold over his followers during the summer of 1903, when the group spent much of the summer on an island not far from Corvallis. (*Seattle Times, *13 July 1906)*

Hubbard" dresses which were ankle-length with full skirts gathered into narrow yokes with long sleeves and high necklines. They went barefooted and bareheaded, with their hair hanging down their backs at a time when women wore their hair pinned high on their head.[17]

Creffield led his followers in long fasts and instructed them to shun unbelievers. Rumors began to circulate that he had a hypnotic influence over the young women in his flock.

Despite some misgivings, the people of Corvallis generally ignored Creffield and his followers during the summer of 1903. The Corvallis *Gazette* ignored the sect altogether, and the *Times* provided just one short article that summer in which it took notice of the conversion of a key Salvation Army officer, Major C. E. Brooks, to the sect:

It is said that the conversion of Brooks was quite spectacular, that in his spiritual excitement he saw and described the devil approaching enwrapped in a network of snakes, and having frogs, lizards and other hideous reptiles clinging to his body; that as a means of placating his devilish majesty he tore off his Salvation Army cap and coat and hurled them into the fire. Then he swooned and became oblivious to his surroundings, an incident common to the rites of the sect.[18]

The *Times* concluded with a backhanded defense of the group, commenting, "This new order is apparently very devout, but their customs, rites and formalities so queer and unusual that the organization has been the subject of much comment from those who do not enter fully into the idea of allowing persons to worship God in the manner that seems to them best."[19]

During the summer of 1903, opposition to the Creffieldites likely was limited because the sect was quite small, little was known about it, and its removal from town meant that Corvallisites didn't have to listen to noisy services all night long. Beyond that, Creffield and his followers may have escaped overt hostility because what little was known about them did not seem entirely out of line with recent developments in American religion. Creffield and his followers were caught up in a wave of religious enthusiasm—called "come-outism"—that was engulfing much of American Protestantism at that time.

Beginning in the 1880s, some American Protestants embraced a holiness movement that emphasized Biblical literalism, high emotion, antagonism toward established churches, and a fervent belief in a "second blessing" in Christian experience. The more radical holiness followers came to believe that traditional, established churches had become so indulgent and sinful that they were beyond reform, thus justifying a decision to leave ("come out" from) those churches for less structured congregations or groups. As historian Robert Anderson writes, the "absolutist mentality" of many holiness people viewed all compromise as sin, all organization as self-serving, and any restraint in worship as anti-Christian. "For them, only a dramatic Christianity of intense emotion could be satisfying." There was little enthusiasm among established churches for this impulse; indeed, the more traditional churches had everything to lose in the "come out" movement, and so denounced the renegades for false beliefs. They also mocked their rolling on the floor, a habit that gave rise to the epithet "Holy Roller."[20] The Creffieldites shared the key traits of Holy Roller come-outism. For the Corvallis *Times*, even though the sect was unusual in its practices, it was to be tolerated as an example of freedom of religion. That tolerance, however, would evaporate in the next few months.

"Positively No Admittance, Except on God's Business"

In late October 1903, the town's somewhat grudging tolerance of Creffield and his followers came to an abrupt end. It was a collision of cultures and beliefs that seemed destined to occur, particularly as the townspeople could no longer ignore the increasingly extravagant behavior of the sect. Moreover, the Creffieldites, although few in number, seemed to threaten the bedrock beliefs and grandiose dreams of the town itself. It became clear to many in town that it was time for Creffield to depart.

The first step toward the collision came when the Creffieldites moved back into town. During the summer, on their island in the Willamette, they had been proverbially out of sight and out of mind. In the autumn, however, now headquartered at O. V. Hurt's new house on the south side of town, the members of the sect resumed the noisy rituals that had bothered their neighbors in the spring. Moreover, they created a new rite that so stunned and shocked the town that hostility was inevitable.

On Wednesday, October 28, 1903, Creffield and his followers emerged into the yard of the Hurt house and proceeded to destroy almost everything in sight. They pulled up the wooden sidewalks and uprooted flowers, plants, and trees. To these they added furniture they dragged from the house, creating a huge pile which they then set on fire. Heeding Creffield's dictum that they could be sanctified only by purging themselves of worldly comforts and possessions, they created a massive bonfire that consumed their goods and shocked the entire town.[21]

Fire always struck terror into small towns in that era, and Corvallis had suffered its share of disaster from fire over the years. Even more troubling, however, this fire had been purposely set, ostensibly for religious purposes, and it consumed a host of useful goods: furniture, carpets, curtains, lamps, bedding, and clothes. For a town of many modest homes and limited incomes, such destruction was simply stupefying. So too was the news that O. V. Hurt, a well-known and respected businessman, seemed so taken with religious enthusiasm that he refused to return to his job at Kline's department store. He sent a messenger to the store to announce that he was withdrawing from the world to devote himself to the work of God. A sign posted on the gate to the Hurt yard warned, "Positively no admittance, except on God's business." A similar sign was posted on the porch, near the front door.

The bonfire attracted widespread attention. Many Corvallisites came by the Hurt home to survey the destruction and wait for the next frenzied burst of activity. That Wednesday evening, about 200 people came by the house—they simply had to see the spectacle for themselves. Those expecting further activity were disappointed: by 8:30 P.M., lights were turned off in the house, and by 11 P.M. the crowds had dispersed.

For the next three days, the town remained stunned by the bizarre doings in the yard of the Hurt home—and by curiosity and dread about what might be going on behind its closed doors and covered windows. The bonfire was the talk of the town. After the initial flurry of pyromaniacal activity, the inhabitants of the Hurt house were still, fueling concern and a host of rumors.

On Thursday, local officials decided to intervene, in an effort to restore order and quiet to the town. The Benton County sheriff, M. P. Burnett, and the deputy prosecuting attorney, Edwin Bryson, visited the house in an effort to talk to O. V. Hurt. They found the front gate wired shut and were forced to climb the fence. When they knocked on the front door, they were greeted by Creffield himself, who refused to let them enter, saying that Hurt was engaged in prayer. The officers told Creffield that they represented the law, but Creffield said he would need to consult with God about them. As Creffield was pacing on the porch, apparently talking to God, bystanders shouted to the law officers that Hurt had come into the side yard, so they abandoned Creffield to talk to the home's owner. Hurt told the officers that there were no problems.

By Thursday evening, the crowds outside the house had grown substantially larger. Some estimated that as many as 1,500 to 2,000 people were milling about—in a town with a population of only 1,800. (Even if estimates of the crowd's size were inflated, it's clear that much of the town was all but transfixed by the odd events at the Hurt home). By now, rumors had circulated that cats and dogs had been sacrificed in the bonfire, though O. V. Hurt himself denied the charge, saying that only one dog—which was already dead—had been burned. Still, some neighbors claimed they had seen the animal sacrifices, and such talk inflamed many Corvallisites. Shortly after dark on Thursday, a few spectators became violent, throwing rocks on the roof of the house and shattering windows. Two men knocked on the front door, and when they were ignored, they broke the glass out of the door. The attacks were limited, however, and after a few hours the onlookers once again dispersed.

On Friday, the outbreak of religious frenzy widened. Early that morning, residents on the north side of Corvallis were awakened by a fire in the backyard of the Burt and Donna Starr home. Rushing to the aid of their neighbors at 4 A.M., people soon discovered that the blaze was yet another Creffield-induced sacrificial bonfire, with chairs, carpets, and clothing put to the torch. Creffield's influence seemed not to be as isolated as some had thought. The sheriff, realizing that angry townspeople might soon attack Creffield, subjected Creffield and his chief lieutenant, Brooks, to a sanity hearing on Friday afternoon that was headed by two local physicians and supervised by the town's deputy prosecuting attorney. After nearly five hours, the two men were released, as their questioners had not found grounds to commit them to the state asylum. As he was escorting them out of the county jail, a deputy sheriff warned Creffield and Brooks that they faced grave danger from angry residents. They dismissed his warning, saying that the Lord would take care of his own.

In a further effort to prevent violence, the sheriff spent Friday night at the Hurt home. O. V. Hurt had demanded protection following the rock-throwing incident on Thursday evening, threatening to contact the governor if the sheriff did not protect him and his family. The sheriff acquiesced, but only after pointing out that the problem was not the angry crowd but the recalcitrant Creffield.

By Saturday morning, perhaps spurred by the sheriff's advice or by rumors that some townspeople were planning to tar and feather the two "apostles," Creffield and Brooks decided to leave the Hurt home.

They waited until later in the day, however, because they feared the crowds milling around the house. By early evening, the crowds had all but disappeared. Brooks left first, walking briskly away from the house; Creffield left a little bit later in a carriage driven by Hurt's son, Fred.

The November 4, 1903, issue of the Corvallis *Times* announced the news:

FLIGHT OF THE 'APOSTLES'

THEY SCENTED DANGER AND HURRIEDLY
DESERTED THEIR BAND OF LOCAL ROLLERS

The paper noted that local "sinners" suggested that Creffield and Brooks had received "a message from on High for them to go hence," but that most Corvallisites believed that the pair simply were afraid of the town's anger. The paper reported that "it is certain that there was a well defined purpose on the part of a body of determined persons to seek the apostles out, to take them across the Willamette, to tell them to clear out, and then if they hesitated or neglected to obey orders, to administer tar and feathers." The *Times* observed that "The flight of the apostles, however, prevented trouble and the public mind is again at rest. With the other members of the sect, nobody so far as is known has any quarrel." With the departure of the sect's leaders, the newspaper and the townspeople of Corvallis hoped for a return to quieter times, free of Creffield's ruinous influence on his followers and free from the notoriety that his antics had brought to the town. That view was overly optimistic.

2 The Shame of Corvallis

Let us keep our shame to ourselves.

—CORVALLIS *GAZETTE*, NOVEMBER 10, 1903

*Corvallis stands face to face with the greatest opportunities within
her history. It is highly essential that matters should be so conducted
as to get the very most out of whatever growth the future may afford.*

—CORVALLIS *TIMES*, MAY 13, 1903

T HROUGHOUT LATE OCTOBER and early November 1903,
amidst all the turmoil generated by Creffield and his followers,
the Corvallis *Gazette* remained remarkably silent about the cult's
activities. Nowhere in that paper was there any mention of the bonfires or of the fact that the town had become truly obsessed with Creffield and his followers. Instead, the paper provided its usual coverage
of Corvallis, replete with accounts of women's church fellowships,
agricultural news, and local business activities. Reading the *Gazette*
provides no information at all about the events that were dominating
town life.

Finally, two weeks after the bonfires and a full ten days after Creffield's flight, the *Gazette* explained its silence. A November 10 editorial
contended that news about Creffield should not be printed because it
was so shameful to the town:

> Let us keep our shame to ourselves, and tell the world what we
> are doing that is creditable to us and our city. When a disgrace-

ful event occurs, it becomes well known in town in a few hours. We don't want outsiders to know about it. It's none of their business anyhow.

Why should the city hide its "shame"? As the *Gazette*'s editorial argued, the news about Creffield would hurt the town's reputation and derail its ambitions for growth and economic development:

> We want good citizens to come to our town and county, to settle and build homes, and support our merchants and our schools. That's the reason we refuse to chronicle the fanatical foolishness, like the Holy Rollers, or samples of youthful depravity that sometimes occur. It accomplishes no good, it caters only to a depraved curiosity and it works a permanent injury to our city. We stand for the advancement of Corvallis, in population, in financial standing, in all that goes to make it larger, stronger, and better.

The editorial concluded with this admonition: "Loyalty to your state, loyalty to your county, loyalty to your town, should be the motto of every citizen."

The *Gazette*'s efforts to hide the Creffield story were futile, but they reflected the great threat that Creffield seemed to pose to the reputation and ambitions of the town of Corvallis. There was some foundation to the *Gazette*'s fears: within days, other Oregon newspapers sensationalized an already sensational story, reporting on the burning of cats and dogs and suggesting that even human sacrifice might be imminent. These papers gave great attention to Corvallis's misery, and some even mocked the town. The *Gazette* complained that newspapers in the nearby rival town of Albany "have considerable to say about our Holy Rollers, but fail to mention her own holy rollers." In an article titled "What Our Neighbors Think of Us," the *Gazette* complained that the Salem *Journal* had called the Corvallis football team "the Holy Rollers" and discussed the "foibles" of Corvallis's citizens. The *Gazette* also noted the Eugene *Register*'s comments about the "scandal that has made Corvallis the subject of much ridicule," and the Albany *Democrat*'s observation that Corvallis "should have muzzled her reporters and kept the thing silent." Corvallis's other newspaper, the *Times,* also lamented the bad publicity. It noted that "the late eruption among the Holy Rollers" had attracted attention all over the United States. "Coast and Eastern papers are beginning to arrive with full accounts of the destruction of furniture and clothing and the burning of cats and dogs." The paper noted that a Corvallis resident had received a letter from a friend in California, asking "what kind of religion the people up in Corvallis practiced" and wondering if his friend had joined. The *Times* lamented, "It is doubtful if any outbreak of religious enthusiasts at any time in the past, especially in which so few people were involved, has attracted such wide attention and comment."[1]

This unwanted publicity and ridicule, coupled with the deeply unsettling practices of the Creffieldites themselves, led the town, and particularly the *Gazette* and the *Times,* to become increasingly hostile to the tiny band of "God's Anointed." No longer would the *Times* defend the group's odd religious practices, as it had once done, under the broad notion of freedom of religion. Creffield and his followers had become an acute embarrassment for the town, making a mockery of Corvallis's efforts to lure new settlers eager to live in a town with bedrock traditional values of family, work, and religion. The *Gazette* and the *Times* would now take the lead in the town's battle against Creffield. They did much to shape the events of the next few years, helping to create an environment in which cold-blooded murder would seem an appropriate, even heroic, action.

The Corvallis Press

The role of the *Times* and the *Gazette* in the Creffield affair was made possible by their particular power and influence in the town of Corvallis. They provided the most important public forum in the community, and the chief source—beyond word of mouth—of news and information. Like small-town newspapers throughout the country, they did much to articulate and reinforce the town's values and to shape public opinion.

The people of Corvallis expected their newspapers to take a leadership role in the community. As was typical among small-town newspapers in the nineteenth and early twentieth centuries, both papers had strong political affiliations: the *Times* served as the Democratic paper for Corvallis and surrounding Benton County, and the *Gazette* as the Republican paper. Each party saw its newspaper as a critical vehicle for party propaganda and as the best way to influence public opinion and arouse the party faithful to show up at the polls on election day. Both newspapers wore their partisan affiliations proudly, and both editors did all they could do to support their parties and candidates.[2]

The papers appealed to readers primarily on the basis of partisanship. The Republican *Gazette,* for example, promised its readers a picture of President Theodore Roosevelt when they paid their subscriptions, and each paper published its party's list of candidates at election time. The *Gazette* ran profiles of Republican party candidates, lauding their intelligence and efficiency. It referred to one candidate for sheriff as "one of Benton county's most promising young men. . . . In Mr. Pell, the republicans have as their candidate for the office of sheriff a young man of force and energy, honorable, industrious and capable, and in every way especially fitted for the position." The *Gazette* also exhorted local citizens to vote for the entire Republican ticket, decrying "a namby-pamby sentiment that it is little difference who is chosen to the several county officers for 'there's no politics in them.' This foolish sentimentality has kept democrats in the most important and lucrative county offices to the exclusion of equally as competent and worthy republicans." The *Times* in turn taunted the *Gazette* for purported inconsistencies in its politics, publicized Democratic party leaders' meetings, and endorsed Democratic candidates.[3]

Parties reciprocated by supporting their newspapers through subscriptions and through limited but important patronage printing jobs, such as county legal notices. This system of advocacy and patronage guaranteed the existence of two twice-weekly newspapers, even though both had relatively small circulations—the *Times* had 1,200 paying subscribers, the *Gazette* 750. It also guaranteed a press actively seeking to lead and influence its community.[4]

Editorial advocacy focused not just on elections and candidates, but also on a variety of local issues. The *Times* and the *Gazette* both supported proposals to improve the community, including electrification, more frequent train service, and better water service. The *Gazette* asserted that electrification would support the town's businesses, and urged residents "to grasp this new proposed electric current as quickly as possible." The *Times* argued that the town needed to agitate for increased train service, saying that it "would be one of the very best things that could happen to Corvallis." Both papers also carried editorials on morals and morality, with the *Gazette* attacking wife beating and the *Times* advocating quick action by local officials against drunkenness and disorderly conduct. In 1903, the *Times* praised a group of local men who had broken up a group of drunken Portlanders who were visiting Corvallis. The paper noted that the local men—"among the town's most respectable and quiet citizens"—had been forced to take the law into their own hands to maintain "the usual dignity and peace of the town."[5]

Apart from their political differences, the *Times* and the *Gazette* were very much alike. Both were small publications, averaging just four pages an edition, and paid attention to local views and events. Both devoted about half of each edition to lists of local events and people. Typical content, from the *Times*'s "Local Lore" section on August 27, 1902, included items such as

Mark McAllister returned to his home in Salem yesterday, after a brief visit with Corvallis friends.

A portion of the machinery has arrived for the proposed steam laundry. Mr. Thompson expects to have the establishment ready for business within a month.

Her friends gave Miss Gladys Moore a surprise party at the home of her mother, Mrs. Sarah Moore, on Third Street on Saturday evening. About twenty young people were present.

New wheat in considerable quantities is arriving at local mills. The price is 53 cents, with only a few small lots reported sold.

The *Gazette*'s "Local and Personal" section on December 13, 1904, included

Judge Hamilton began a term of court at Toledo yesterday.

Henry Robinson is quite ill at his home in this city.

J. A. Archibald was in the city from Philomath last Friday.

J. W. Buster, of Alsea, was a visitor in Corvallis last Friday and Saturday.

Although the editors of the papers provided extensive editorial commentary on town and political issues, they did little original news gathering. Instead, the news usually "came" to the newspaper office. Corvallisites themselves submitted many of the accounts of local events that were published in the Corvallis press; the *Gazette* editor reminded his readers to be sure to write legibly so that he could get the facts correct. The secretary or recorder for local groups, such as the town's improvement association, a woman's church auxiliary, or a local Masonic lodge, wrote up meeting minutes and gave them to the papers for publication. Area residents routinely dropped by the newspaper offices to "report" or comment on local events. After an area farmer visited the *Times*'s office, the paper ran an article about his views on a proposed state appropriation for the upcoming Lewis and Clark Exposition. The paper invited others to send in their views. On another occasion, a city council member stopped by the office, and the result was an article on issues facing the council.[6] On another occasion, the *Times* editor reminded his readers that he merely was repeating what his visitor had told him:

> Dick Dunn has furnished the Times with a bit of Kings Valley news, but the paper does not want to vouch for its reliability. Dick once reported the birth of a child to an aged couple to whom such a thing had not previously happened, and in fact, had not happened then.[7]

This emphasis on local news, often supplied by Corvallisites themselves, meant that the *Times* and the *Gazette* provided rich detail on the town and its residents—houses bought and sold, the condition of crops and businesses, visitors, new residents, social events, births and deaths. No topic seemed insignificant if it had touched the life of at least one resident. The Corvallis press had close ties to its readers, cemented first by political affiliation, and second by attention to the details of everyday life.

While the *Times* and the *Gazette* retained much of the partisanship and local focus common to nineteenth-century U.S. newspapers, they also reflected the increasingly commercial character of the U.S. press of that era. Both papers turned increasingly to advertising as a key source of revenue, thus tying the papers more closely to local business interests. Both ran many columns of advertisements for local merchants, and local businesses and their owners received substantial and usually favorable news coverage. For example, when the local livery stable got a new coat of paint, the *Times* noted that "the improvement adds much to the appearance of the premises."[8]

The *Times* regularly promoted new businesses—such as a furniture factory, a laundry, and a carriage factory—urging local residents to patronize those establishments and thus improve the town's economy. In an editorial in 1902, the *Times* urged Corvallisites "to become patrons of the local enterprise. The way to build up a town is to patronize those in it." When the new laundry was started, the paper observed that the quality of work was good and prices were low; "they deserve the laundry work that Corvallis has to bestow, much of which now goes abroad." When the Hotel Corvallis opened in 1903, the *Times* bragged that the building was what one would expect "in a goodly city, rather than in an ordinary college town." When a new dry goods store opened in town, the *Gazette* noted the store's excellent stock, gushing that "It was like a fairyland within." The *Gazette* gave extensive coverage to S. L. Kline, owner of a local dry goods store and a prominent Republican leader in the county, publishing his observations from travels around the country.[9] For both papers, what was good for business was good for Corvallis.

With their close ties to the local political and business establishment, it is no surprise that both the *Times* and the *Gazette* were ardent supporters of efforts to attract newcomers. In 1901, in an article titled "What Immigration Could Do," the *Times* noted that population growth would benefit everyone in the town by increasing land values and creating prosperity. The *Gazette* took a similar stance, and both papers often framed their discussion of local issues in the context of luring newcomers. When the county government erased its debt and thus eased the local tax burden, the *Times* heralded the occasion, adding, "Newcomers may make a note of the fact." The *Times* supported creation of a new town water system, quoting one expert who claimed that "if once established, it would do more to attract people to Corvallis than would any other single influence that can be named." Ever mindful that other towns were trying to attract settlers, too, the *Gazette* championed the granting of a franchise to developers of a new electricity system for the city, saying that it would "put us on a par with our sister towns throughout the valley."[10]

Both papers characterized the local Oregon Agricultural College as a great benefit to the town and as an inducement to new settlers. The *Gazette* called the college "the pride of our people. It is the biggest thing in town, in fact, the largest college in the state and the greatest Agricultural College on the coast." The *Times* quoted one local businessman who said: "I personally know that when newcomers arrive here looking for a new location, that the very first thing they admire is the Agricultural College, and that they are at once in many instances, seized with a desire to locate near it so they may educate their sons and daughters."[11]

The *Times* ran testimonials from settlers extolling the many virtues of the town and the surrounding region. On one occasion, it quoted a recent immigrant from Iowa who said, "I have kicked myself many a time for not leaving Iowa and coming here twenty years ago."[12] The *Times* also portrayed Corvallis as a pleasant place to live—a town with good homes and an active and highly moral citizenry:

> The streets are broad and well kept and bordered with ribbons of green and embowered with shapely trees. Cozy cottages and handsome homes are found in the resident district which form the border of substantial brick business blocks, giving the city the general appearance of solidity and commercial activity. Civic and fraternal societies are well represented while the many church organizations are in a flourishing condition. The public school system is of the best and the people take a pardonable pride in their temples of wisdom.[13]

Both newspapers provided leadership in the immigration effort, giving residents advice on how to improve the town to make it more attractive to newcomers. The *Gazette* urged the townspeople to clean up their yards, streets, and alleys to give a "favorable impression" to visitors from the National Grange in November of 1904. "There will be people here from every state of the Union and we should strive to give them a favorable impression of our really pretty little city. The best way to do this is to clean up the alleys, streets and private premises in the city. The court house janitor gives a good demonstration of how this can be done. Let public officers and our citizens generally, find a hint there and go and do likewise." The *Times* also told the townspeople to clean up their yards. "The constant coming of newcomers on the hunt for new homes has occasioned the general desire for better appearances." It also urged local voters to support a ballot measure for new school construction, arguing that new schools were absolutely essential for success in attracting new settlers.[14]

The *Times* also contended that Corvallis would fail in its efforts to grow if it didn't improve its sidewalks; the paper noted that a businessman visiting town had commented that other towns in the Willamette Valley all had far better sidewalks. On another occasion, the paper urged Corvallisites to attend the dedication of the new Agricultural Hall at the Oregon Agricultural College. A large turnout of local residents, the paper pointed out, would impress the important visitors (including the governor) who were coming for the ceremony; "upon the impressions they receive will depend much of weal or woe for Oregon Agricultural College, for Corvallis and Benton [County]."[15] Contending that Corvallis needed better train service, the *Times* asked local leaders to petition the Southern Pacific Railway to offer an additional train each day:

> It is still true as it was when Noah's ark floated on the flood, that an isolated town is a dead town. It will continue to be true until Gabriel blows his trumpet at the crack of doom. In these days of quick transit and lightning changes, live men won't wait forever for a chance to go somewhere. They settle in towns where there is a chance to get out and get in, and that's the biggest of all drawbacks to Corvallis.[16]

Both papers were optimistic that Corvallis, with its rich agricultural land and a welcoming spirit, would succeed in drawing newcomers, who in turn would provide the foundation for great economic growth and prosperity. In May 1903, the *Times* proudly stated that the town "stood face to face with the greatest opportunities within her history." But such an opportunity could be squandered, the paper warned, so "It is highly essential that matters should be so conducted as to get the very most out of whatever growth the future may afford." The "unwise or unprogressive shaping of local affairs" could undermine the town's momentum and prevent growth:

> Hindrances could be set up that could for years arrest progress. Things can be left undone to prevent the proposed era of development and growth. From whatever standpoint considered, it is easy to see that the present and the immediate future is a crucial and most important moment in the career of the municipality.[17]

The *Times* wasn't alluding to Creffield in that warning in May—he had not yet registered as a potential problem. Within just a few months, however, he had very clearly emerged as just the kind of hindrance that could "for years arrest progress," and both the *Times* and the *Gazette* became virulent opponents of Creffield and his teachings. The position of these newspapers would be extraordinarily important in the months and years ahead, as they provided leadership in shaping town opinion and action.

The Corvallis Press and Creffield

In covering Creffield, the two Corvallis editors took on the typical role of small-town newspapers of that era, primarily providing their views rather than a dispassionate rendering of the facts. There was little need for them to report the facts of the Creffieldites' activities—in small towns such as Corvallis, the news of events such as the bonfire spread rapidly just through word of mouth. As the *Times* recounted, "On the streets . . . no other topic was discussed. Men stood in groups on the pavement and related incidents concerning the sect or expressed opinions of what should be done."[18] In the Creffield case, the editors provided what they regularly gave to their readers: analysis, commentary, and opinion.

The *Times* and the *Gazette* were, first and foremost, advocates for their town and its values. The newspapers were long accustomed to their role as leaders of public opinion, and their increasingly strong denunciations of Creffield did much to legitimize violence against him. They also reassured their readers that the fault was not in Corvallisites but in "outsiders" such as Creffield who preyed on emotionally weak women. Repeatedly they told their readers that the town's problems would evaporate if Creffield just left Corvallis.

Both papers were fairly unified in their views on Creffield; only occasionally did their coverage hint at their longstanding political differences. The Democratic *Times* noted that Creffield's host in Corvallis was none other than O. V. Hurt, a leading Republican official whose involvement "has added unusual impetus to the sensational character" of the cult's actions."[19] The *Gazette*, a Republican paper, did not mention that detail.

In its first coverage of the bonfire at the Hurt home, the Corvallis *Times* was not particularly hostile to the Creffieldites, describing them in terms no stronger than "annoying," "peculiar," and "fanatic." The paper saved its greatest criticism for those who had thrown rocks at the Hurt home and broken several windows. It called the stoning "a contemptible outrage" and lamented that the identity of the rock throwers was unknown. "All the acts were wanton, excuseless and brutal, and the perpetrators should be sought out and punished."[20] With this stance, the paper made clear its defense of the law, and thus helped prevent escalating violence against Creffield and his followers.

Within five days—on November 4, 1903—stung by mounting bad publicity throughout the state and appalled by Creffield's teachings, the *Times* took a much more critical view of the Holy Roller leader in its next issue. No longer was Creffield or the sect merely "annoying" or "peculiar," and the threat of violence against him was no longer condemned as "a contemptible outrage." Instead, the paper noted that people had good reason to be extremely angry at Creffield for "leading women, girls and others into delusions and unnatural conditions" and threatening to break up families. Creffield—"a stranger"— was undermining the traditional values of the town. This was a significant shift for the *Times*; it was a leading voice in the town, and its increasingly strident criticism of Creffield would help to legitimize not only the grievances against the Holy Roller leader but also retaliation against him.

The *Times* presented a bleak picture of Creffield. It admitted that the facts in the case were not entirely known—whether Creffield had preached against marriage was not known, and the full extent of family disruption in town was still unclear. But the trajectory of his teachings was clear: this outsider was destroying entire families.

> Another feature that the public resented was that in which wives and daughters in the home joined the sect and other members of the family did not. The teaching of the apostles is that the members of the sect are withdrawn from the world and must have nothing to do with those who remain in the world. . . . A bitter alternative was necessarily left to the husband whose wife was in the sect and he was not. She was out of the world, and he was of the earth, and she would have nothing to do with him.[21]

In lawyerly fashion, the *Times* examined the potential defenses that might be presented to justify the Creffieldites' practices, and found them wanting. The editor reminded his readers that he believed fervently in freedom of religion, even if that religious practice was ridiculed by those who did not share the same beliefs. Burning furniture and household goods might be defensible, if done in a spirit of true belief. But genuine religion never endangered its followers, and here Creffield had clearly transgressed. The *Times* told its readers that Creffield had preyed on weak-minded women, leading them into folly and delusion. In a stirring indictment of Creffield and his teachings, the paper denied that it was "proper worship" to stir "persons of moderate mental vigor . . . into false positions." Nor was it proper worship to play "upon the minds in such way that there is delusion and folly." The paper stressed that Creffield and Brooks were both strangers in the community—"almost wholly unknown"—who were "leading weak women into a state of mind where there is more frenzy than reason, more folly than sense."

> If these comparative strangers, who call themselves apostles and claim to hold constant communication with the Almighty are

subsisting wholly on their labor of leading women and young girls into delusions and unnatural conditions, and if in pursuit of that labor home times are wrecked and happiness driven away from firesides, great and irreparable wrong is committed.[22]

Based on this analysis, the *Times* concluded that violence against Creffield might well be the only way to rid Corvallis of this menace. The newspaper noted that the threat of violence ("many a reference to tar and feathers, to vigilance committees") against Creffield and Brooks had forced them to flee—and the paper most emphatically cheered their departure. "The flight of the apostles, however, prevented trouble, and the public mind is again at rest. With the other members of the sect, nobody so far as is known has any quarrel."[23]

Both the *Times* and the *Gazette* held out the possibility of violence if Creffield and his followers disrupted the town again. The *Times* warned that if Creffield returned and further religious frenzy ensued, retaliation could be expected. The *Gazette*—having abandoned its strategy of trying to avoid publicizing Creffield's actions—took a stronger stance, noting that violence against the apostles, although ideally to be avoided, would be "deserved." The *Gazette* added, "It is but right, however, to warn these people that a single overt act on their part will be a signal for prompt and effective measures to rid Corvallis of a nuisance, and that will be a lesson to future Rollers and howlers, as they will do well to note."[24]

Creffield and Brooks returned to the Hurt home in early November, but they and their followers kept a very low profile. Times had changed, however, and within a few weeks O. V. Hurt told the two self-styled apostles to leave his home. Even though his wife, son, and daughter still remained loyal to Creffield, Hurt had had enough. With Hurt's protection and prestige withdrawn, many believed the Holy Rollers would leave town for good. The *Gazette* editorialized, "The citizens of Corvallis are to be congratulated on the fact that the Holy Roller craze in this city is a closed incident, and will not appear again in the news from our city." The paper was pleased that "the Holy Rollers have passed forever into history." The *Times* reported that "their departure this time is for good and aye," and noted that there was "a return of all interested to normal conditions. . . . The friends of Mr. Hurt and of the family are glad that Creffield and Brooks are gone, for to the latter and their power to influence others was due whatever there was in the late matter that supplied the public with things to talk about."[25]

Between late October and late November, there had been a radical change in public opinion in Corvallis, and the *Gazette* and *Times* had done much to lead that change. An awestruck town had stared in puzzlement at the burning of furniture and household goods, but few had done more than talk about driving the sect leaders out of town. By late November, Creffield and Brooks had lost their host in town, and were facing a much more hostile public mood. That mood was driven in part by embarrassment at all the bad publicity and in part by mounting outrage at Creffield's unseemly hold on young women.

But what helped it all jell, what helped legitimize this growing anger was the position of the town's two papers. The shift in their positions was remarkable and significant. In late October, when the Creffieldites had first shocked the town with their bonfire, the *Gazette* had tried to ignore the issue completely, while the *Times* had dismissed it as "annoying" and had criticized those who harassed the sect members. Within a short period of time, however, these important Corvallis institutions had issued a public indictment of the leaders of "God's Anointed" and declared them personae non gratae. Both editors declared that the sect did not represent legitimate religion, that, indeed, it posed a danger to the mental health and morals of its followers. Most importantly, the newspapers excused vigilante activity against the two cult leaders, contending that their actions invited violent response. The stinging indictments of Creffield and Brooks in the *Times* and *Gazette,* coupled with the newspapers' tolerance of retaliation, went far toward creating an environment in which violence against the two sect leaders was seen as appropriate—or even justified.

Within this environment, retaliation against the sect's leaders became all but inevitable if they remained in town and continued in their unorthodox ways. They were persistent, however: although both Creffield and Brooks left town in late November, they didn't go far. They set up headquarters at a house just across the Mary River from Corvallis. There they continued their prayers and incantations, and there they were rousted out by vigilantes on the night of January 4,

1904, tarred and feathered, and ordered to leave Corvallis forever.

The story of the events of that night is fairly simple. A crowd of about twenty Corvallis men assembled on Main Street around 9 P.M. and crossed the river by ferry. They surrounded the house where Creffield and Brooks were staying, broke down the front door, and took Creffield and Brooks—tied together—back across the river and then north of town. The vigilantes ordered them to remove their clothes, tarred and feathered them, and told them they would face more drastic treatment if they ever returned to Corvallis.[26]

The more interesting story of that night is that of the vigilantes themselves. The group included leading citizens of the town, and they made no effort to hide their actions. As the Corvallis *Times* recounted:

> There was no attempt at secrecy by those who took part in the affair. None wore masks and none affected a disguise. The identity of many of the party is known, and these are men of standing and character . . . not a boy or hoodlum in the party.[27]

They marched Creffield and Brooks through town right on Main Street, highly visible for all to see under the electric streetlights.

Among the vigilantes was B. F. Irvine, editor of the Corvallis *Times*. He later provided an eyewitness account for his readers, describing the barefooted Creffieldites and their reaction to the intrusion:

> At the sudden appearance of the intruders, the members of the sect were more or less startled. Brooks and Creffield were at once ordered to put on their shoes. It was, however, apparent that they were not astonished, having lived no doubt in the expectation that something of the kind was likely to occur at any time. The female portion of the assembly began to sing, and so continued during the rest of the ceremony.[28]

Irvine also described the scene north of town, where the vigilantes tarred and feathered their victims, in vivid detail:

> The scene at the moment was unquestionably dramatic. The moon shone clear and bright in the eastern sky. The two apos-

tles nude and shivering in the center of the group. Silence was only broken by the movements of the men and by an occasional remark, sometimes of a jocular character. One man, surveying Creffield, after his head and body had been well smeared with the tar and feathers, remarked, "Well you would make a fine old Santa Claus now." The apostle made no reply. All the time he trembled like an aspen, and was undoubtedly much frightened. It was otherwise with Brooks, who was stoical throughout and apparently undisturbed by the proceedings.[29]

Irvine defended the vigilante action against Creffield and Brooks; it was illegal, he noted, but justifiable. All of the vigilantes were known to the public, he wrote; all were guilty of a misdemeanor, but none would ever be charged. "The reason is that the two men had committed offenses against the people of the vicinity that the law could not reach." He intoned the town's grievances against the Holy Roller leaders, referring to both the unwelcome notoriety and the moral outrage:

For weeks the community has been made notorious by the fool acts of the zealots and their half crazed followers. A system of religion was set up in which this pair of high priests and their followers worshipped behind barred doors and closely drawn blinds, behind which the public could neither pass nor see. Though a shock to the proprieties, it was alleged worship of Almighty God for these two huskies to live in the same locked house with a number of young girls, and do nothing in the world but be religious. Whether as fools or knaves, whether as fanatical zealots or as sinister hypocrites, it remains a fact that the acts of Creffield and Brooks, practiced under any other name than that of religion would have led to violent scandals and an interference by the public on the grounds of common decency long ago.[30]

Irvine added that the Holy Roller leaders—and Creffield in particular—had led to "a succession of disagreeable as well as deplorable occurrences and conditions, such as no community deserves, and as few would so long tolerate."[31]

The *Gazette* also defended the vigilantes, echoing the *Times*'s argument that the action was made necessary by the inadequacy of the law. The *Gazette* noted that virtually all Oregon newspapers had expressed their views on the tarring and feathering episode. Some praised the vigilantes while others condemned them, and to the latter, the *Gazette* retorted: "Put yourselves in our place!"[32]

The popularity of the vigilante activity was noted by the state's leading paper, the Portland *Oregonian*. It observed that it was impossible to find anyone in Corvallis—except perhaps for a few deluded fanatics—who condemned the violence against Creffield and Brooks. Indeed, not only was there no opposition, but there was enormous support for the vigilantes. The *Oregonian* cited the "many outspoken expressions of approval" that showed "a drift of public sentiment that cannot be misunderstood." With the ringleaders gone, "several persons of the gentler sex" had calmed down. The *Oregonian* predicted that the nightmare was over: "It is altogether likely that Corvallis is not to be disturbed again with the sensations in its religious world that have made the town so prominent during the last few weeks." The Salem *Statesman* agreed that the vigilante action against Creffield and Brooks had been necessary, saying, "it would be difficult to conceive a more appropriate punishment for the persistent indulgence of their idiotic and disgusting antics in the name of religion."[33]

Corvallis was truly rid of Brooks. In late January, 1904, he was part of a very small Holy Roller camp that was run out of Linn County by the sheriff. Brooks and two others had been camped out in the woods near Lebanon, Oregon, and area residents at first suspected the band of being robbers who had recently struck at nearby towns. Consequently, several police officers and farmers surrounded the camp, armed with shotguns and other firearms, only to discover not robbers but Holy Rollers reading their Bibles. The police ordered them to move on; they protested against moving on a Sunday but were given no choice.[34] The Linn County episode was the last account of Brooks' activities; after that, he disappeared from the attention of Corvallis citizens.

The Corvallis *Times* was confident that Creffield was gone for good, too. It commented, "It is very probable that the events of the last week will put an end to the Holy Roller movements as recently conducted in this vicinity." The paper reiterated the town's grievances against the self-styled apostles, noting that "to them is ascribed all the blame for such undesirable notoriety as has come upon the community." The "discipline" administered to Creffield and Brooks had helped bring sanity back to the town and had calmed the overly emotional women who had followed the sect leaders. This was the "end of Holy Rollerism hereabouts."[35]

But Holy Rollerism wasn't gone, despite the actions of the town's vigilantes. Creffield would continue to haunt the town, continue to inspire young women, and continue to flout the moral norms of the town. Following the tarring and feathering in early January 1904, however, a clear consensus marked the town's attitude toward Edmund Creffield. As articulated in the *Times* and the *Gazette*, the townspeople saw Creffield as a distinct threat to the town's hopes of progress. If the law could not prevent his activities, then it was the duty of honorable men—acting on their own—to do what was right.

3 Weak Women

But justice is above law, and a relative of one of those victims has the undoubted right to claim reparation for this crime even to the taking of life.

—CORVALLIS *GAZETTE*, JANUARY 12, 1904

The husbands or brothers of these misguided women who run after this fakir seem to have something lacking in their make up, or the Holy Roller would long ere this have been given a treatment which would have prevented him from carrying out a portion of the religious rite which he is accused of practicing on his victims.

—PORTLAND *OREGONIAN*, MAY 3, 1906

THE TUMULT CAUSED BY CREFFIELD and his followers brought great embarrassment to the town of Corvallis, and this helped to fuel the town's anger toward him. Even more upsetting, however, was the concern that Creffield was immorally exploiting emotionally vulnerable young women. This threat soon became seen as Creffield's primary offense, justifying revenge in the name of honor.

In the Corvallis press, the indictment of Creffield knit together a series of attitudes and grievances: Creffield was an outsider whose hypnotic power easily seduced women. These women were not to blame for their misguided devotion to him, because by nature they were weak creatures easily led astray. Creffield's success with them served to reinforce the traditional view of women's inherent mental fragility and the belief that only men could protect women from the vicissitudes of the world. For the press, both in Corvallis and elsewhere, the apparent failure of the law to stop Creffield further underscored the need for men to exercise their role as benevolent protectors.

In contrast, the women who followed Creffield did not see themselves as weak women who needed to be protected from him or from their own emotional or physical frailties. Indeed, they exhibited both fortitude and endurance in the pursuit of their beliefs. They readily abandoned the protection of their families and many of life's comforts, eating only minimally or not at all, praying for many hours, living at times out of doors. Despite widespread criticism and forced institutionalization, they persisted in their devotion to Creffield and to his teachings. In some contexts, such devotion might be seen as a sign of great moral and physical strength, or even of divine calling. Given the unorthodox nature of Creffield's teachings, however, their devotion was broadly construed as insane rather than heroic.

"Weak Women"

A host of late-nineteenth- and early-twentieth-century publications—advice books, medical treatises, magazines, and newspapers—all promulgated the notion that women had fairly circumscribed roles in society. Duties and competence all centered on the home and family, and other endeavors or occupations were seen as only serving to exacerbate women's inherently fragile mental and emotional makeup.

Advice manuals, an important form of popular media throughout the nineteenth and early twentieth centuries, often stressed that the proper role of women was as wife, mother, and homemaker. In *Ideal Married Life: A Book for All Husbands and Wives*, physician Mary Wood-Allen argued that women make the home, which is central to society, marriage, and family. "The home is the wife's domain." Robert F. Horton, an English writer whose advice books were reprinted in the United States, also stressed the importance of the home. A young wife, he wrote, "brings all her powers to build the home, to deck it with beauty, to grace it with thought and feeling." Clara Jessup Moore, a prolific writer of advice books under her own name and under the pen name of Mrs. Bloomfield H. Moore, declared in her 1892 *Social*

Ethics and Society Duties that the "true woman" was "the faithful wife and devoted mother, whose life is passed in the holy and tender ministries of home."[1]

Other advice manuals warned that women who sought careers outside of motherhood and home would be vainly challenging their natural abilities and temperament. In *Talks to Young Women,* published in 1897, Charles Parkhurst warned of the dangers facing women if they spurned their role in the home. "God and nature" had given women their mission, and "any feminine attempt to mutiny against wifehood, motherhood and domestic 'limitations' is a hopeless and rather imbecile attempt to escape the inevitable." The result, he warned, would be "irreparable injury" to the woman; motherhood gave women as wide a sphere as they needed or were capable of filling.[2]

One writer in *The Independent* argued in 1905 that women were physically and mentally inferior to men in the workplace. Substituting women for men in an office setting, for example, required a larger staff because women "are less rapid than men, less able to undertake the higher grade work, less able to exert authority over others, more lacking both in initiative and in endurance, while they require more sick leave and lose interest and energy for marriage." Another magazine writer in the early 1900s contended that women had weaker nervous systems than men, that they were equipped for a placid life, and more demanding situations would undermine their health quickly. Many medical experts believed that a woman's body was prone to diseases, including insanity. A well-known medical expert of the era, S. Weir Mitchell, pronounced that "The man who does not know sick women does not know women."[3]

The problem was considered to be primarily their sexual physiology. The cause of a woman's supposed debility, both physical and mental, was a reproductive/sexual system that purportedly dominated her life, drained her energy and left her susceptible to a host of physical and mental problems. Many physicians and scientists of the time believed that bodies had a finite amount of energy, so women's mental growth slowed with the onset of puberty as their reproductive organs matured. Puberty, according to some experts, also created a hypersensitivity whereby girls became "as susceptible to external influences as the barometer to atmosphere changes." As such, young women were advised to take great care during puberty; in 1901, Dr. Mary Wood-Allen advised women to avoid physical or mental exertion during puberty. In preparation for that challenge, she advised that girls "should cultivate a serene spirit and strong self-control at all times." But puberty was just the start of a long period of mental and nervous debility; many physicians also believed that a woman's "periodical ordeal" left her further susceptible to hysteria, listlessness, or insanity—what one writer referred to as the "temporary insanity of menstruation." The belief that women were more susceptible than men to disease, that they were predisposed to insanity, and that the cause was their reproductive system, persisted despite the lack of proof. As historian Sheila Rothman notes, this view of women's weakness was a common part of popular discourse. "A host of popular magazines and newspapers spread these notions, especially through their advertising columns. No group more consistently preached the doctrine of women at risk than the patent medicine industry. Medicine manufacturers defined menstruation as an illness, and a serious one." The leading psychiatrist of the era, Isaac Ray, was certain that women's extreme nervous susceptibility easily led to hysteria and insanity.[4] Within this worldview, women's perceived disability gave men a particularly important role as guardians and protectors.

The Corvallis Press and Women's Roles

Like most media of the era, the Corvallis *Times* and *Gazette* both presented a very traditional view of women as daughters, mothers, and wives who should be devoted to family and home. The *Gazette* approvingly quoted a traveling lecturer who described the modern woman not in terms of suffrage or independence but as a person who remembered her obligations to family and home:

> To the woman, he paid the highest tribute, but he also talked plainly to her. The "coming woman" he declared to be the one who reigned as queen in her home. One who did not shift the responsibilities of her household to other shoulders in order to indulge in the vanities of life.[5]

As represented in the *Times* and the *Gazette*, Corvallis women fit this role as the "queen" of the home. Neither newspaper mentioned, much less supported, woman suffrage in 1903, and nowhere was there evidence that women's role in society might be changing—or even that this role was under discussion. The women of Corvallis, as they were depicted in the *Times* and the *Gazette*, were devoted homemakers who cooked and cleaned for their husbands and children. They kept their homes neat, and cared about the appearance of their families and themselves.[6]

According to the local press, Corvallis women were active in their churches, for which they hosted suppers, organized donations for foreign missions, held bake sales, and sang in the choir. The *Gazette* publicized an upcoming sale by the Ladies Aid Society of the United Evangelical Church, noting that "They are making every effort to provide good things to eat and will have on hand many useful articles. They are busy as bees." Many of the town's women belonged to a church social group, meeting every month for lunch or refreshments and an inspirational program. Women were also caregivers—the *Times* reported that a local woman had gone to Dallas to care for her ill father, while another woman had just returned from an extended visit to care for her brother. The leading "public" organization in Corvallis was the Coffee Club, established to provide coffee for firefighters and later expanded to include projects such as beautification of the town. In 1906, for example, the Coffee Club was leading the city in creating flower beds.[7]

For Creffield's female followers, however, living up to these much-valued traditional roles was virtually impossible. They abandoned their mainstream churches for frenzied worship led by Creffield, and their constant praying left them little time for household chores. Moreover, Creffield forbade the women to share company with any who did not belong to their little band, so some of the women abandoned their roles as homemakers and nurturers, refusing to cook for their families and shunning sexual relations with their husbands. Creffield's admonition to his followers to forsake worldly comforts led them to neglect their personal appearance; the *Gazette* reported that some of Creffield's women devotees appeared in public without a hat (contrary to custom) and, worse yet, with their hair unkempt.[8] Burning household goods in bonfires, of course, ran contrary to any definition of domesticity.

In early November, the Corvallis *Times* excoriated Creffield for "leading weak women into a state of mind where there is more frenzy than reason." The paper warned that "great and irreparable harm" would come from leading "women and young girls into delusions and unnatural conditions"; the result would be that "home ties are wrecked and happiness driven away from firesides." The *Times* also noted that one young Corvallis woman—a Creffield follower—had been confined to bed due to "intense nervous and mental excitement." Following the tar-and-feather attack on Creffield and Brooks in early 1904, the *Times* reiterated its claims that the chief victims of Creffield were unstable women, condemning the cult "officered by two ornery galoots, founded by nobody and followed only by women." One woman had already been sent to a Portland sanitarium, the paper noted, and another half-dozen women in Corvallis were suffering from "nervous shocks and mental agitation" so acute that they had "wounds that will never heal."[9]

Weak women and opportunistic fanatics: that became the Creffield story in the Corvallis press during the weeks and months ahead. This story provided a framework for attacking Creffield while allowing forgiveness of his followers. Weak by nature, women were not free agents in whatever choices they made about religion, and so were not to blame for taking part in dubious or even sordid activities. The blame belonged instead to the male outsiders—"comparative strangers"— who were exploiting women's inherent weaknesses. Within this calculus, it was the duty of the "stronger sex" to protect and defend women. The Corvallis *Gazette* first explicitly made just such an argument in early 1904. Frustrated with the law's inability to punish Creffield, the newspaper endorsed the notion of honor killings—that relatives of the young women led morally astray by Creffield had the right to kill him as retribution for the ruination of the young women. "But justice is above law, and a relative of one of those victims has the undoubted right to claim reparation for this crime even to the taking of life."[10]

Where Is Creffield?

Between early 1904 and 1906, the Creffield saga went through periods of drama and calm, depending on Creffield's activities. It was a period of mounting frustration for many, and particularly for families who found it virtually impossible to free their daughters, sisters, or wives from Creffield's influence. Each "recovery" was only temporary—the women seemed perpetually vulnerable to the zealot's power. The law had been unable to stop Creffield from exploiting these "weak women," and vigilante justice increasingly held out the only promise of an end to the Holy Roller nightmare. The press contributed to this mounting impatience with the legal system, inflaming public passion by vilifying Creffield and urging more drastic action against him.

After the tarring and feathering in early January 1904, Creffield dropped out of sight, but he left the town with much to talk about. On the day after the incident, he married Maud Hurt, daughter of O. V. Hurt, in nearby Albany. Maud returned to her father's home in Corvallis, and locals began tracking her movements but never spotted Creffield. For her part, Maud refused to talk to reporters or others about her new husband. Rumors persisted that he was living in the nearby woods, sending missives to his followers. Still, the town was relatively calm; Creffield's Corvallis devotees apparently stopped their troubling behaviors and returned to their usual churches and family duties.

Unable to meet with his Corvallis devotees, Creffield soon headed to Portland, where he had once lived while working for the Salvation Army. Creffield may have gravitated to Portland because Esther Mitchell was there. Esther had become one of Creffield's most ardent followers during the summer of 1903. Just fifteen years old, a quiet and fairly withdrawn girl, she had readily joined in the extended, emotional rituals of the sect, and she seemed particularly taken by the charismatic Creffield—and he with her. Her brothers George and Perry, alarmed at Creffield's influence over Esther, sent her to Portland to live with friends shortly after the bonfire episode. She ran away immediately, finding her way back to Corvallis and to Creffield's fold. At that point, in mid-November 1903, her brothers forcibly returned her to Portland, sending her to the Boys and Girls Aid Society Home. Despite its benevolent-sounding name, the home was essentially a detention center, where Esther would be kept away from Creffield and, her brothers hoped, her infatuation with him would run its course.[11]

Creffield's continued interest in Esther Mitchell was matched only by her passionate loyalty to him. Indeed, her persistent devotion worried the officials at the Boys and Girls Aid Society Home in Portland as much as it did her brothers. Officials at the home later recounted her avid—even frenetic—Bible reading, which seemed to upset her so much that officials confiscated her Bible. They also attempted to limit visits from Esther's sister, Donna, who clearly was encouraging Esther in her loyalty to Creffield. Both women were persistent. Donna once snuck into the home by crawling through a cellar window, and attendants found her and Esther in Esther's room, locked in embrace, shouting their prayers: "Glory to God! Down with the Devil! Victory! Victory!"[12]

Esther's brother, George, believed it was his duty to protect his emotionally vulnerable sister from Creffield and his suggestions. He did all he could to keep her away from Creffield, but his efforts only alienated Esther. The two had never been particularly close; he had been just twelve years old and Esther eight when their mother died and Esther went to live with another family. Still, George felt a parental responsibility for Esther, particularly since their father had remarried and moved to Illinois. George went to Portland and warned the officials at the Boys and Girls Aid Society Home that Creffield or one of his cohorts—most likely Frank Hurt—would try to free Esther from the home. George was deeply distraught by his younger sister's religious frenzy; it pained him so much that he did not want to see her. Home officials later reported that he said, "No I cannot stand to see her. I never want to see her in that condition."[13] Worried that Creffield might somehow free Esther from the home, George sent her to Illinois in early February 1904, to live with their father.[14] He fervently hoped that such distance would free her from Creffield's grip.

Unable to get at Esther, Creffield turned his attention to her sister, Donna. The mother of three small children, she was married to Burgess (Burt) Starr, also a former Corvallis resident. After his wife joined the Creffieldites in 1903, Burt had moved the family to Portland. Away from Creffield, Donna had apparently returned to a more normal life.

Now, in early 1904, Creffield was back, and Donna soon fell under his influence again.

With a few other devotees, they resumed their religious practices in the Starr home, shouting, singing, and rolling. Creffield had also developed a rite for purifying souls through sexual intercourse, and created what he called the Church of the Bride of Christ. Finally, Burt Starr could take no more; Donna's participation in Creffield's "purification rite" led Burt to file a criminal complaint of adultery against Creffield in Portland at the Multnomah County District Attorney's office.

Once again, the law seemed inadequate in stopping Creffield; he escaped arrest by going into hiding. Portland police occasionally thought they knew his whereabouts, but were unsuccessful in apprehending him. The Corvallis *Times* reported that townspeople were worried he might surface again, so they had raised a $100 reward for his capture. The paper reminded its readers of Creffield's destructive influence on Corvallis families: "Nearly all of the sum was contributed by husbands whose families are or have been identified with the Rollers."[15]

Although Creffield could not be found, he once again began to influence his Corvallis devotees. Frank Hurt—Creffield's sole remaining male follower—appeared one day at the Corvallis post office without hat, shoes, or socks, wearing just a light shirt and overalls. Deeming him unbalanced, local law officials attempted to capture him, but he fled across the river to Linn County, where he lived. On May 3, 1904, the Corvallis *Gazette* reported that some of Creffield's female followers were once more defying conventional modes of dress, appearing on the streets "with unkempt hair and without wraps to protect them from the chilly air." The light dresses the women wore were considered immodest—particularly in public—reinforcing the sense that Creffield had undermined traditional morality. Once again, women stopped carrying out their traditional family duties as wives or daughters, refusing to cook for their families or to speak to nonbelievers. The *Oregonian* later noted that "the misery and sorrow incident to these conditions was far beyond the public conception of it. Wives denied the husbandship of their husbands, refused to speak to them, denied all relation with them, went shoeless and hatless, and but poorly clad."[16] O. V. Hurt later described his wife's actions:

"I hate you, but I love Creffield," my wife told me when I expostulated with her because of her conduct. I begged and I pleaded, but it was of no use. She would listen to no argument. She wouldn't even take care of the adopted child. I cared for it in the morning, dressed it and looked after it until I left the house. Then I took it to a neighbors and left it there until I returned home. My wife and my daughters refused to wash the child's clothing or to wash its body. They refused to feed it, or to wash the dishes in which the baby's food was prepared. They declared that God would be displeased with them if they had anything to do with the child. Creffield had told them so.[17]

The Corvallis *Gazette*, outraged at this new outbreak of Holy Rollerism, indicated that the town was quite eager to settle up with Creffield. The paper told its readers that dire action would be justified; "something probably will be done," the paper noted, because Creffield was "a menace to young women." Frustration was acute because law-enforcement officials could not find the Holy Roller leader. The sheriff flooded the county with wanted posters, searches were made of homes in the area, and Corvallisites had taken to tracking Maud Creffield's every move.[18] Creffield was not to be found, and still managed somehow to choreograph his followers' behavior. He seemed remarkably skillful at making a mockery of the legal system.

Unable to solve their problem by confronting Creffield, Corvallisites decided to take drastic action against his followers by committing them to the state asylum for treatment. Until now, residents had generally excused the devotees as mentally and emotionally weak folk who would ideally "recover" with Creffield's absence. Now, even with Creffield nowhere in sight, they still seemed under the zealot's hypnotic spell. O. V. Hurt and others hoped that treatment in the state asylum would return the devotees to calmer and more socially acceptable behavior.

Six people—five women, one man—were sent to the state asylum in Salem, and another three women went to the Oregon Boys and Girls Aid Society Home in Portland. O. V. Hurt said he decided to commit four of his family members because he had been "driven to distraction" by their odd behavior. Such commitments were procedurally easy—a family member's request needed verification only from a single local physician. At the commitment hearing for O. V. Hurt's son Frank and Frank's wife, Olive, the elder Hurt was the key witness. He described the couple's refusal to work and their destruction of good clothing and other property. Frank admitted that he had burned his good clothes "on orders from God" and that he had destroyed a new bicycle for the same reason.[19]

Most of Creffield's followers were committed without incident; Sarah (Mrs. O. V.) Hurt was the exception. As O. V. Hurt later recounted, "When the sheriff came for my wife, she refused to leave. She fought with all her strength, and declined to clothe herself sufficiently to permit of her removal. By brute strength we put a suit of union underwear on her and other garments. She tore them off and when she was carried from the house, still fighting, the lower portion of the union suit had been torn loose and was wrapped about her neck."[20]

The Corvallis *Gazette* justified the commitments, stressing that the "law abiding" citizens of the city wanted rid of "this foolish outfit." "If there were no other reasons for sending them away, their reckless disregard for decency and the sanctity of the home would be just and sufficient cause." The *Gazette* also stressed the emotional vulnerability of "sensitive" people who had been "led astray" by Creffield.[21]

Over the course of the next two years, the notion of insanity as regarded the Creffieldites would become an elastic concept, stretched one way or the other to justify retaliation against Creffield and his followers. It was invoked repeatedly as a way of controlling women who acted outside social norms, but never applied to Creffield himself, despite ample evidence of mental imbalance. This type of effort to control the women was not altogether unusual for that era; the behavior of women who challenged social norms at the turn of the century was often interpreted as evidence of mental instability. Historians Gamwell and Tomes note that "the reinvigoration of the women's suffrage movement in the 1880s and 1890s only heightened anxieties about the so-called new woman. With growing frequency, medical arguments linked women's allegedly unnatural activities outside the home with both diminished mental stability and reproductive capacity." Although some women physicians challenged this view, "the idea that overtaxing the female brain resulted in both insanity and degeneration of the human species remained very common in medical circles at the turn of the century." Challenging conventional sexual practices was dangerous. In New York, one woman, Lucy Ann Lobdell, was institutionalized in 1880 because she dressed like a man and lived with another woman; she spent the rest of her life, until her death in 1912, in state institutions.[22] Although Creffield's followers did not fit the profile of the "new woman" of that era, they did challenge conventional social norms—and so they soon found themselves inside mental institutions.

Creffield's Arrest and Trial

Unbeknownst to all but a small handful of followers, Creffield had returned to Corvallis and had been living underneath the Hurt family home. From there, he had been giving instructions once again to his devotees, inciting the odd behaviors that had triggered the insanity commitments. As his followers left town, headed for the asylum, Creffield's source of food was soon gone. He was nearly starved when he was discovered one day by O. V. Hurt's young son Roy. The youth had been crawling around under the house when he noticed "something white back in the northeast corner." When he heard a voice speaking in broken English, he concluded it was Creffield. He summoned his father, who in turn contacted the local police chief.[23]

When Creffield finally emerged from under the house, he was emaciated, had a scraggly beard, and could barely stand. The police took him to the county jail and returned him the next day to Portland to stand trial on the adultery charges. Corvallis papers mocked him for hiding under the Hurt home. The *Times* called Creffield a coward: "Any man with the spirit of a seven year old boy in him, would have quit the spot any dark night, and have fled to some other place where at least he could stand on his pins and look at the world in the face." Despite his mocking tone, the editor was still adamant that Creffield had committed terrible wrongs: "Murder, arson, theft, bigamy, burglary, riot, and the ordinary crimes are trifling in their effects on society, compared to the wickedness of Creffield."

By this point, Creffield's mental state seemed precarious. After his capture in Corvallis, he said, "Oh I feel so good, Jesus is so near me, Jesus told me last night this would happen." When he left Corvallis on a train for Portland, he ignored a crowd of onlookers and quietly sang a hymn, "Jesus Hath the Victory."[24] While in jail in Portland, he gave a rare interview to reporters from the *Oregon Journal*. His comments disclosed a troubled mind:

> I am now Joshua, high priest and at some future time, will become Elijah, the restorer. My work is to lead the 13 tribes of Israel back to Jerusalem, where the restoration of all things will take place and the millennium will dawn on earth. I have a mighty work to accomplish. That work I will accomplish as God directs. I cannot know what my lot will be, but whatever comes to me, that will I construe as God's holy will. I went under the Hurt residence at Corvallis not knowing what would befall me. I know now that I was crucified there and my spirit, body, and mind were purified. I now know no sin. I was there prepared for my future work, which I know is to restore Israel to Jerusalem.[25]

In court, Creffield continued to claim that he had been entrusted by God with a holy crusade. He refused the appointment of an attorney, telling one judge that "God will not justify for me to have one."[26]

As speculation mounted in Corvallis and Portland that Creffield was truly mentally imbalanced, the Corvallis *Times* argued that the cult leader should be held fully accountable for his actions and sent to the state prison. The paper warned that anything less, such as sending him to the state asylum, would be a travesty of justice. "If Creffield should, on a subterfuge of lunacy, cheat the penitentiary of its long overdue deserts, indignation in this city would be very much heightened." Creffield acted not out of lunacy, the paper claimed, but from "downright deviltry." It claimed that he had become an adept hypnotist while he was still in the Salvation Army. "There is practically no other explanation by which this insignificant man could gain such control over daughters as to cause them to deny their parents, and such power over wives as to induce them to forswear their own marital relations, treating their own husbands as unworthy and discredited strangers." The *Times* insisted that Creffield's actions were far worse

than the ordinary run of crime. "There is no excuse for him, no pallia-
tion for his offenses, no room for him where there are decent folk to
be pestered, misled and ruined by his practices."[27] The *Times*'s attacks
on Creffield before his trial were quite harsh, and they would only
increase in intensity in the aftermath of the court testimony.

The surprise in Creffield's trial was really no surprise at all. He and
Donna Starr readily admitted what others long had feared: Creffield
had engaged in sexual intercourse with her as part of a purification rite.
What most angered the community—and particularly Corvallisites—
was Creffield's claim that he had acted on God's orders. Justifying
his sexual activities, Creffield claimed that "God teaches that one
must have direct connection with him before he can be saved. . . . God
called me to do all I have done and I am obeying Him. The gospel
He put on me was to purge the body and I have done so. Jesus Christ,
I tell you, has chosen me to purge the flesh from sin of all those who
are willing."[28]

During his testimony, Creffield quoted extensively from the Bible,
asking the jury each time to turn to the passage he was citing. The
Portland *Oregon Journal* reported that "Judge Sears was by this time
scanning the good book closely, evidently impressed with the belief
that that preacher was insane."

Creffield wrapped up his defense by addressing the jury:

> In the eyes of your law, yes, I am guilty. In the eyes of God, I am
> innocent. I know He is on my side. And while you may lock me in
> my prison cell, I can still cry 'Glory to God' and rest secure in the
> knowledge that when the time comes, God will plead my case!

The judge told the jury that Creffield could be acquitted if found
insane, but the jury took just fifteen minutes before it returned with a
guilty verdict. Creffield, seemingly unperturbed, went back to his jail
cell murmuring "Glory to Jesus, Glory to God." Later that same day,
September 16, 1904, the judge sentenced Creffield to the maximum
sentence possible, two years' imprisonment in the state penitentiary.
After the judge pronounced the sentence, Creffield responded, "God
Bless you." By nightfall, he was in the state prison in Salem.

The Inadequacy of the Law

The law had at long last dealt with Creffield, but in Corvallis there was little satisfaction with the verdict. On the contrary, his trial served to further inflame those who despised him. There was really nothing new in what Creffield or Donna Starr had said—rumors about all of this had been circulating for a full year in Corvallis. Still, Creffield not only had expressed no shame but had continued to insist brazenly that he acted at God's bidding. The Corvallis *Times* condemned Creffield as a "scoundrel" who engaged in "depravity" while posing as a saint. "His like in perfidy and dishonor would be hard to duplicate on the face of the earth." Moreover, the Corvallis *Times* contended that Creffield's awful admissions clearly justified the tarring and feathering that had been administered in Corvallis earlier that year, and the paper praised the vigilantes for enormous self-control in not killing him. In ringing terms, the paper characterized Creffield as far worse than the most depraved criminals:

> The man who lies in wait and shoots his victim down is a gentleman compared to this man-shaped reptile. The fire-bug is one of the lowest and most despicable of offenders, but he is even respected compared to this rotten Creffield. The ordinary libertine who enters a home and contaminates it, is vile beyond compare, but his offense is trivial in contrast with that of him who does the same thing on a false pretense of Christianity and with the name of Jesus and God on his dirty lips. In vileness, diabolism and all round deviltry, Creffield is unmatched, and matchless as his own avowals and the desolate condition of his asylum victims so faithfully prove. In his brazen confession, there is full and satisfactory explanation of why those he had wronged drove him, tarred and feathered, from Corvallis, and a wonderful exhibition by them of self control and respect for legal authority, in that they did nothing worse.[29]

The *Times*'s indictment was sweeping. What was a fitting penalty for such transgressions? The paper didn't supply that answer, but it saw the two-year prison sentence as a trivial punishment. The Corvallis *Gazette* echoed the *Times*'s vilification of Creffield, calling him a "bogus prophet of God, religious hypnotist, imposter and all-round dangerous individual." The *Gazette* also felt that the law had failed the people because the two-year maximum sentence was too lenient. "It is not commensurate with the enormity of the crime. The work of this dangerous man has been far more extensive and far-reaching in its results than most people allow themselves to think."[30] Although both papers held back from explicitly urging violence against Creffield, their vilification implicitly argued for just that.

Creffield was in state custody, however, so there was no opportunity for those who wanted stronger retaliation. Once again, a measure of calm returned to Corvallis. When Maud Hurt Creffield was released from the state asylum, she returned to live at her parents' home in Corvallis, and she broke her ties to Creffield by divorcing him. Most of the other Creffieldites who had been sent to the state asylum were released, too, and returned to Corvallis and to ordinary lives. Most of the women so long mesmerized by Creffield returned to local churches that practiced a less frenzied Christianity. In Illinois, Esther Mitchell appeared cured of her obsession with Creffield, so her father allowed her to return to Oregon. She took a job at a mill in Oregon City. Only Sarah Hurt seemed unable to return to a more normal routine; she had been freed from the asylum in early September 1904, shortly before Creffield's trial concluded, but returned there a month later. The Corvallis *Gazette* reported in early October that "her condition is improved but not as much as was hoped for."[31]

Despite its calm surface, Corvallis remained a troubled town. Residents were uneasy about their Holy Roller adventures and worried about their ability to recover. The *Gazette* said that the "stigma" of the insane asylum would never leave those who had been committed, and worried that the "dangerous religious doctrines" would never be completely erased. More importantly, the town faced an uncertain future, the *Gazette* contended. "The very fact that the city of Corvallis has endured him and his sect for so long without making pronounced effort to have them removed has had a baleful and deadening effect on public morality." Nerves remained raw. When Salvation Army members attempted to re-establish a Corvallis mission in late 1905, they were met with outright hostility. Recalling Creffield's background in the Army, the *Gazette* condemned the group as "brazen" for trying to "inflict themselves upon us." It urged the Army to devote its energies to the slums of large cities where they might do good. "Can any person review the history of this organization in Corvallis and say they have not done more harm than good?[32] The *Gazette*'s reaction, perhaps more than anything else, showed the deep anger just below the surface in Corvallis. The Army deserved no blame for Creffield's antics, yet anything reminiscent of the Holy Roller leader was enough to produce great protest from the local press.

In prison, Creffield kept to himself. In a rare article on the cult leader during his prison term, the *Gazette* reported that Creffield talked little, avoided conversation with others, did not try to convert others, and kept quiet about his plans for after his release. "If he feels any degree of disgrace or humiliation, he does not betray it." Creffield volunteered for the road crew, where, as part of a group of closely guarded inmates, he worked in rock quarries mining stone for road surfaces. Once, during a work assignment at the rock quarry near Rosedale, Oregon, he and some members of the road crew attended church services in Rosedale. When the service was opened for testimony, Creffield made an impassioned presentation, demonstrating that he had lost none of his charisma. Work on the road crew was physically taxing and thus not terribly popular among the inmates, so prison officials gave two days' credit on sentences for every day worked on the road crew. With this work, Creffield was able to reduce his two-year sentence considerably, completing his term in about fifteen months. He left the Salem Penitentiary in December 1905. Upon leaving the prison, he traveled to California, visiting Sacramento and San Francisco before returning to Oregon in early 1906.[33]

Creffield's early release and his return to Oregon truly alarmed Corvallisites, who feared that he would once again plunge the town into turmoil. His early release surprised many and underscored the notion that the law was inadequate for dealing with someone as depraved as Creffield. Moreover, he brazenly claimed that he had been "resurrected" while in prison. After O. V. Hurt wrote to him, warning him to stay away from Corvallis, Creffield cautioned Hurt to stay out of his way if Hurt valued his own life. "I have now got my foot on your neck. God has restored me to my own. I will return to

Oregon and gather together all my followers. Place no obstruction in my way or God will smite you." Hurt and other Corvallis residents scrambled to defend their town and homes from Creffield; not only did they keep a close watch on all people coming into town, they also monitored the mail.[34]

Creffield had anticipated all of this, however. He foiled the efforts of Hurt and others by using a go-between to reestablish contact with his Corvallis followers. The emissary was Esther Mitchell, now seventeen, who had remained true to Creffield and was eager to help him. During her time in Illinois, Esther had at first continued her devotion to Creffield, refusing even to speak to her father because he was not a Creffieldite. After several weeks, however, she appeared to have a change of heart. Esther's father had little desire to deal with her, and told her brothers that he was convinced she was "cured" of her religious infatuations. George Mitchell, the brother who had engineered her trip to Illinois to keep her out of Creffield's clutches, was outraged when he learned that Esther had been allowed to return to Oregon. He was convinced that she would eventually fall victim to Creffield again. George railed at his brother Perry, and at his father, telling them that he would never speak to either of them again if anything bad befell Esther. Esther bridled at George's insistence that he knew what was best for her, but George paid her little heed.

Creffield sent letters for his followers to Esther in Oregon City, and she either put them in new envelopes or took them herself to Corvallis. Before long, Creffield had reestablished full communication with his devotees and told them of his plan to set up a colony on the Oregon coast, near Waldport. Waldport is only ninety miles from Corvallis, but it is on the other side of a short coastal range of mountains, and the road west from Corvallis to the coast was rough. Apparently Creffield expected that this relatively remote location would allow him to reassemble his flock without fear of violence from the leading men of Corvallis.

Few of the most faithful could ignore the siren song of Creffield's call. Maud Hurt—who had married Creffield in 1904 and divorced him in 1905 when he was in prison—remarried him in early April.[35] By mid-April 1906, about a dozen of Creffield's followers—again, all women except one—had assembled in the wilds of the Oregon coast, living in tents buffeted by cold winds and soaked by spring squalls. Shortly before Frank Hurt left to join them, his father pleaded with him to stay away from Creffield. "I told him he was crazy to quit his job and leave his home and go out on a career such as that on which he was embarking. He got mad and threatened to have nothing more to do with me. . . . He insisted it was God's desire he should meet Creffield." In Portland, Donna Starr deserted her husband and three small children in the middle of the night. She left a note for her husband, telling him she was taking all the money she could find in the house—about $2.50—and heading out on foot.[36]

The Corvallis *Gazette* was dumbfounded at Creffield's new venture. It "passeth human understanding" how he had ever established his group; now, after a prison sentence, it seemed even more incomprehensible that anyone would follow him anywhere. What was clear, however, was the persistence of Creffield's perfidy: "adultery and Holy Rollerism seem inseparable." The *Gazette* warned the people of Corvallis that they faced the horror of it all once again. It was clear, the paper observed, that the asylum "cure" had been temporary at best; Creffield's devotees were following his call to the coast. "What can be done with or for a people who are so weak as to follow the damnable teachings and practices of a man like Creffield"? The paper urged authorities on the coast to act promptly and to "use every means within their power to protect their people from pollution by Creffield."[37]

Frustrated by what they saw as the failure of the law, and supported by an angry press, several Corvallisites began to take more drastic steps to deal with Creffield. Lewis Hartley tried to stop his wife and daughter from joining Creffield by attempting to force them off the Corvallis-Waldport train. They eluded him, leaving the train partway to the coast and finishing their journey on foot. He continued on to the coast, where he resolved to do what others had been talking about for some time—kill Creffield. In Newport, he bought a gun at a secondhand store. The following day he attempted to shoot Creffield five times, but failed because the cartridges would not fire. Creffield's followers believed this to be a sign of divine protection for the leader. The next day, Hartley set out again to find Creffield, this time carrying a functioning Winchester rifle. For three days he waited near the Rollers' camp, but Creffield had disappeared.[38]

Hartley wasn't the only man trying to kill Creffield. D. H Baldwin, also from Corvallis, spent three days trying to find Creffield. Baldwin's daughter had been an early Creffield devotee, but had seemingly returned to normal while Creffield was in prison. She soon fell under his sway again, and only through force had Baldwin stopped her from joining the camp. He decided that the only way to put a stop to her devotion for Creffield was to kill him.[39] Several other Corvallis men, all armed with guns, also took a train to the coast, hoping to catch Creffield. He eluded them by fleeing on foot to Albany and then north to Seattle by train. Creffield told his followers to await his directions: he would establish a new camp elsewhere and send for them. His opponents, not knowing he had gone on foot, started watching the Corvallis and Albany train stations and searching trains, hoping to capture him. Once again he seemed to have vanished.

George Mitchell joined the ranks of those hunting Creffield in late April and early May 1906. In early April he had been hospitalized in Portland with the measles, and as soon as he got out of the hospital he learned of Creffield's "resurrection" and of his two sisters' decision to join the coastal camp. The news that Donna had deserted her family in the middle of the night was a severe blow to Mitchell. Burt Starr, Donna's husband, recounted later, "George took my little ones on his knees and wept while he caressed them and told them that he would go and bring their mother back." Starr later commented that he had become alarmed by Mitchell's brooding about his sisters, and particularly by his conviction that Esther would become Creffield's next sexual conquest.[40]

Mitchell spent several days in Corvallis, checking trains from the coast and talking to O. V. Hurt and to some of the other men who had been hunting Creffield. As he talked, he heard more and more about Creffield's sordid activities and became increasingly convinced that Creffield must die. Failing to find Creffield, he followed Maud Hurt from Corvallis to Albany and then to Portland. In Albany, Maud was warned that he had been following her; she recognized him but did nothing to avoid him. Mitchell thought he lost sight of her in Portland, but he finally caught a glimpse of her boarding a train to Seattle. Mitchell followed the next day. He arrived in Seattle on Wednesday, May 2, 1906, and began hunting for Maud and Creffield.[41]

The day after Mitchell's arrival in Seattle, an editorial in Oregon's leading newspaper, the Portland *Oregonian*, revealed just how serious the Creffield situation had become. The newspaper bleakly described the continuing Creffield problem: he was at large and continuing to undermine the emotional and moral health of young women. The paper contended that Creffield's continued freedom would only lead more women to the asylum; he was busy "accumulating another stock of lunatics who sooner or later will have to be taken care of by the state." What was most significant in the *Oregonian*'s editorial was its clear endorsement of vigilante violence against Creffield. The responsibility for action, the paper said, belonged to the families of the weak women Creffield had misled. The editorial pointedly criticized the men in those families for failing to take decisive action against Creffield:

> The husbands or brothers of these misguided women who run after this fakir seem to have something lacking in their make up, or the Holy Roller would long ere this have been given a treatment which would have prevented him from carrying out a portion of the religious rite which he is accused of practicing on his victims.[42]

In such an environment, with the state's leading newspaper abandoning the legal process and castigating husbands and brothers for not taking decisive action, Creffield was living on borrowed time.

4 The Press Proclaims a Hero

I did only what any true brother would do.

—GEORGE MITCHELL

Mitchell did a good deed.

—CORVALLIS *GAZETTE*, JUNE 26, 1906

O N MAY 7, 1906, the first edition of the daily Seattle *Star* broke the news of a sensational murder. A young Oregonian, George Mitchell, had shot and killed Edmund Creffield on a downtown Seattle street early that morning. In police custody, Mitchell had calmly admitted his guilt:

"I GOT MY MAN; AM IN JAIL."--

BROTHER SLAYS MAN WHO RUINED SISTERS

"HE RUINED MY TWO SISTERS AND I TOOK HIS LIFE"--GEO. MITCHELL

George Mitchell Shoots and Instantly Kills Edmund Creffield, Leader of Fanatical Religious Sect--Victim Accomplished Ruin of Slayer's Sisters---Avenger Followed His Man For Weeks and Is Now Satisfied.

GEORGE MITCHELL
Slayer of Frank Edmund Creffield.

The *Seattle Times* that same day also trumpeted the news:

CREFFIELD SHOT TO DEATH

LEADER OF NOTORIOUS HOLY ROLLERS INSTANTLY KILLED BY YOUNG MAN WHOSE SISTERS HE HAD LED ASTRAY

Self-Styled Apostle Meets a Tragic End at Hands of George Mitchell, Who Long Ago Had Sworn Revenge

Both newspapers recounted the chief facts of the May 7 shooting. While searching the downtown Seattle streets for his prey, Mitchell saw Edmund and Maud walking toward him shortly after 7 A.M. Backing into a recessed doorway, Mitchell waited until they walked past him, then leaped out, half-yelled, "Creffield," and shot a .22-caliber pistol point-blank at Creffield's head. The Holy Roller leader slumped to the ground, killed instantaneously. There were no witnesses, save Maud, who shouted at Mitchell, "He never did you any wrong." Several men nearby heard the shot and hurried to the scene, but Mitchell made no effort to flee. The police soon arrived, finding Creffield dead, his wife in shock, and Mitchell calmly lighting a cigar. He quietly surrendered, voluntarily handing his gun to an officer. From the jail in Seattle, he sent a telegram to O. V. Hurt in Corvallis, saying, "I got my man. Am now in jail."[1]

The newspapers' accounts of the killing, though, were just the tip of the proverbial iceberg. Over the next five weeks, between the shooting on May 7 and the beginning of George Mitchell's trial for murder on June 25, the *Star* and the *Seattle Times* vied with each other in telling the shocking and scandalous story of Edmund Creffield and his followers. The result was a public-relations campaign so impressive and far-reaching that many Seattleites—including dozens of prospective jurors—were soon convinced that the man in custody was an enormously brave and virtuous avenger of wronged womanhood. He did not deserve the death penalty, but rather had earned the thanks and praise of a grateful society.

Together the *Times* and the *Star* presented a heart-wrenching account of the sordid excesses of Edmund Creffield, all the while praising George Mitchell as the only man brave and determined enough to put a stop to such wrongs. By the time Mitchell's trial for murder was to start, these papers had so successfully attacked Creffield that the dead prophet, rather than Mitchell, had become the real villain of the story. The key legal facts in the case—that Mitchell had, with premeditation, shot Creffield in cold blood—were obscured by thousands of words describing Creffield's sordid activities.

The role of the *Times* and the *Star* was significant, particularly because it helped defeat local law-enforcement officials who hoped to convict Mitchell of first-degree murder, a capital offense. King County Prosecutor Kenneth Mackintosh believed that the facts demonstrated a clear-cut case of premeditated murder, so he filed charges against Mitchell and vowed "to prosecute the defendant fearlessly and vigorously." Joining Mackintosh in his denunciation of Mitchell was John F. Miller, his chief deputy. Miller contended that the shooting of Creffield was "the worst murder that has been committed since I have been in Seattle."[2]

In the battle between prosecutors and press for public opinion, the press emerged triumphant for several reasons. To start with, it presented a picture of George Mitchell that was entirely consonant with broader cultural values. By invoking themes of weak women and brave men, and of men's duty to protect the honor of women, the press coverage resonated with a wide range of commonly held beliefs of that era. The press gave an enormous amount of coverage to the Mitchell-Creffield case in May and June 1906, often providing front-page banner headlines, articles, and photographs. It would have been difficult for the average newspaper reader not to know about the case. Furthermore, mass media are powerful institutions; they do not just provide "the facts" in a case such as this one, but can also impart a broader set of judgments about what is right or wrong, good or bad.[3] In this case, through the selective and often emotional coverage provided, the newspapers presented the virtually inescapable conclusion that Creffield was the real villain and Mitchell a hero.

Urban Journalism in the Early 1900s

Press coverage of this story in Seattle, and particularly by the two rival afternoon newspapers, the *Seattle Times* and the *Star*, was shaped not just by the story at hand but by the broader profile of journalism in the early 1900s. Urban newspapers of that era were a fascinating jumble of news, entertainment, and advertising. Their most notable characteristic was their diverse content; the traditional journalistic staples of news about politics and business were now crowded by articles about theater, sports, fashion, and society, and by comics and advice columns.

Such diversity was propelled by publishers' never-ending quest for greater circulation. One newspaper industry trade journal of the time declared that the modern newspaper had become like a menu at a great hotel restaurant—no guest expected to eat everything available, but they valued their many options. "One reader turns to the stock market, another to politics, another to baseball, another to book reviews, another to musical and theatrical notices, another to a sermon or lecture." This mindset propelled editors to offer a vast array of content to their varied readers. As the editor of the Pittsburgh *Leader* bragged in the late 1890s, "No matter in what you are interested, you will find the subject of your hobby duly exploited[4] . . . in fact, whatever you most like to read, you will find the Leader's departments are the most carefully prepared, the most complete and the most interesting."[5]

Circulation's allure was primarily economic. Even at two or three cents per copy, newspaper sales could generate significant revenue for a newspaper. More importantly, though, circulation drove advertising, which soon emerged as the newspapers' chief source of revenue. Advertisers saw newspapers as an effective way to reach consumers, and as today, the larger the circulation, the more advertisers were likely to pay for space. A writer in the *Newspaper Maker*, another newspaper industry trade journal, noted that publishers wanted their circulation to grow because "The larger he can make the figures which the sales show, the broader the basis on which he may adjust his rate card."[6]

In this bigger-is-better environment, newspaper owners and their editors were not particularly shy in courting readers. They ran contests (such as "favorite preacher") and offered premiums (such as free books, plants, or dolls) to create excitement about their papers. They regularly engaged in crusades on a variety of community issues, replete with vivid headlines and prose. They seized upon sensational events, such as the Mitchell case, knowing full well that such cases would boost circulation. Newspaper tycoons such as Joseph Pulitzer in St. Louis and William Randolph Hearst in San Francisco in the 1880s (and both in New York City in the 1890s) demonstrated clearly the circulation gains that followed news coverage of crime, passion, and tragedy. Around the country, editors noticed and copied that formula.

Editors also learned that a well-told tale, replete with heroes and villains, pathos and drama, could enthrall readers and drive daily sales. Interviews added immediacy and personality, and drew still more readers. No subject was too humble; indeed, many editors found that some of the most poignant prose could be written not about presidents or kings but about simple folk—immigrants, working girls, orphans. The *Seattle Times*, for instance, ran a story in 1906 about a Chicago orphan whom no one would adopt because his "poor, little stunted body" discouraged potential adopters. He never lost hope, though, and greeted each visitor to the orphanage, saying, "Aren't you going to 'dopt me?" The article also told of the competition among the orphaned boys whenever a visitor came calling; their acrobatic stunts and other feats seldom overcame the overwhelming preference for adopting young girls.[7]

News writing was an amalgam of fact and opinion in the early twentieth century. Although editors by 1900 had ostensibly separated "news" from "opinion" by establishing a formal editorial page, the selection and play of news still often reflected the political views of newspaper publishers and owners. Newspapers owned by E. W. Scripps, for instance, regularly ran crusades against local monopolies (in utilities, street railways, ice, coal, etc.), which reflected Scripps's ardent embrace of a general Progressive reform view. The pursuit of the well-told tale also led to opinionated writing and moralizing. Many reporters and editors, lacking formal training in journalism or ethics, prized colorful writing over impartiality.

Journalism in Seattle

In Seattle, the *Times* was the foremost example of the new urban journalism. It was an oversized broadsheet publication, running eighteen or twenty pages on weekdays and three times as many on Sundays.

The paper touted its diverse content with front-page notices:[8]

THE TIMES IS THE ONLY PAPER THAT PRINTS
A COMPLETE WOMEN'S SECTION

TWO SHORT STORIES AND A NOVEL IN THE SUNDAY TIMES

On May 1, 1906, the *Times* bragged that its entire print run from the preceding Sunday had been sold out: "The circulation of the Seattle Sunday Times last Sunday was 54,275 copies—and the newsboys had cleaned the office completely out before 9 o'clock." A few days later, the *Times* bragged that it carried more advertising and printed more pages than the morning *Post-Intelligencer*. "What better proof does anybody need of the complete supremacy of *The Times* over the *PI,* than the foregoing facts?"[9]

The *Times* offered its readers a wide variety of content: national and international news, local happenings, sports, fashion, news about the theater—and it did all of this with great gusto, reflecting the advice of its owner, Alden Blethen, "to raise hell and sell newspapers."[10] Blethen, owner and publisher of the *Seattle Times* since 1896, relished his paper's high profile in Seattle. In just ten years, he had established it as a vibrant presence in the city, dedicated to many populist and Progressive causes and generally supporting a mixture of working-class and middle-class interests.

The *Times* was also brash, loud, and often sensationalistic. In May 1906, for example, it engaged in a war of words with California Governor George Pardee. A *Times* reporter, Robert Boyce, had been dispatched to California to cover the aftermath of the San Francisco earthquake; he reported that Pardee had terribly mismanaged the disaster and was so unpopular he would never win reelection. When Pardee purportedly telegraphed Blethen to complain about Boyce's article and the "sanity of your news editor for having printed it," the *Times* gave extensive coverage to the issue. In a front-page article, the *Times* said it had "never yet found Mr. Boyce unreliable," and then reprinted the original story to allow readers to choose between the governor and the reporter. The headline included the *Times*'s colorful retort:[11]

SOME DOUBT EXISTS AS TO THE SANITY OF ONE OR MORE OF THE TIMES' EDITORS, BUT NONE AS TO PARDEE

The next day, the *Times* continued the battle with a front-page headline:

CALIFORNIA'S CHIEF EXECUTIVE, WRITHING UNDER REALIZATION OF POLITICAL RUIN TRIES TO DISCREDIT CHARGES . . .
FLIES IN FACE OF INDISPUTABLE EVIDENCE IN FRANTIC ENDEAVOR TO REMOVE DISGRACE FROM POLITICAL SUPPORTERS

The corresponding article typified the vivid news-writing style of the *Times* and of many urban newspapers of the era:

> Tottering on his unstable pedestal of governorship, George C. Pardee, chief executive of the State of California, is venting his puerile spleen upon The Seattle Times, which through interviews and by its special representative in San Francisco has given publicity to the unheard of conditions existing in the stricken city.[12]

The paper also printed, on its front page, photos of "Gov. Pardee and Four Seattle Men Who Disagree With Him" and ran statements from the four Seattleites (including business leader Jacob Furth and local prosecutor Kenneth Mackintosh) supporting the *Times*'s assessment that a "reign of terror" had arisen in San Francisco. The *Times* ran three banner headlines that day, all about the dispute:[13]

PARDEE GETS AFTER MACKINTOSH!

GOVERNOR TAKES EXCEPTIONS TO LATTER'S CRITICISMS!

JACOB FURTHER BACKS UP BOYCE'S STATEMENTS!

The other Seattle afternoon newspaper, the *Star,* was part of the growing E. W. Scripps newspaper chain. Like other Scripps newspapers, the *Star* was a low-budget operation with a news staff of just six reporters (half the number of the *Times*'s staff).[14] Realizing that his little papers could not match their competitors in general news coverage, Scripps instructed his editors to differentiate themselves from their competitors; as a result, his newspapers focused extensively on working-class issues and human-interest stories.

Scripps's focus on the working class reflected his dedication to social justice, but it was also a carefully crafted business strategy designed to build circulation among a segment of the population often ignored by mainstream newspapers. He told one of his editors that "every page and every article" in a Scripps newspaper should reflect the interests of the common people. "Hook yourself tight and close to the heart of the common people. Be always with them and of them."[15]

Scripps also thought that human-interest articles built circulation far better than any other kind of content, so he exhorted his editors to fill their columns with stories that had a compelling emotional element. He believed that the public read newspapers "largely to pass time or to kill time," so the true test of an editor was his ability to provide content that pleased such an audience. "Sensational matter is absolutely essential to a newspaper," he insisted, defining sensationalism as "that kind of matter which produces some sensation of humor, of indignation or gratified curiosity or any other sort of sensation." In practical terms, Scripps and his executives urged his newspaper staffs to use vivid language and headlines and a wide variety of entertaining material—including comics, inspirational editorials, short stories, and articles about odd events or unusual people. For current news, he and his editor-in-chief, Robert F. Paine, urged their editors to provide "news features"—that is, the interesting stories behind the news. The emphasis was less on getting the news first and more on presenting the news in an interesting fashion.[16]

Scripps's Seattle newspaper, the *Star,* carried out its owner's orders well. It was a vigorous defender of working-class interests, crusading for pure food and milk, collective bargaining, direct election of U.S. senators, and a host of other Progressive-era reforms. It also presented the news in a distinctly vivid and compelling manner, often casting the news as a struggle between the good (the workers, the "Common People") and voracious monopolists (including John D. Rockefeller, local street-car and telephone companies, and lumber barons who were gouging the public). It attacked wealthy automobile owners who drove too fast and defended an "aged" local couple evicted by their landlord.[17]

The Mitchell case was an ideal story for both the *Star* and the *Times*. The mixture of murder, a religious cult, and questionable sexual practices made this a riveting and sordid story, which augured well for circulation. The story was also a good fit for the Seattle *Star*'s hero-versus-villain format. Given the highly competitive nature of the afternoon newspaper market in Seattle, both the *Star* and the *Times* were bound to exploit the story as much as they could.

The Canonization of George Mitchell

On the morning of May 7, editors and reporters for the *Seattle Times* and the *Star* quickly realized the potential of the Creffield murder story. Facing first-edition deadlines shortly before noon, and ever aware of their mutual journalistic rivalry, editors from the two newspapers had to scramble to cover the story. Only two people had firsthand knowledge of the crime, and one of them—Maud Hurt Creffield—did not want to talk to reporters. George Mitchell, on the other hand, was happy to talk to reporters; he gave an extensive interview from the county jail just a few hours after shooting Creffield—and just before the reporters' deadlines.

Mitchell played an important part in defining the news story. For all practical purposes, he was the only source the reporters could turn to that morning, so his view of Creffield's actions and of his own motives in killing Creffield were the only ones reporters could get easily and quickly, and he was willing to talk frankly to reporters. The interview was dramatic. Mitchell's stunning admission that he had indeed killed Creffield—and that he was glad he did—was quite unlike the reactions of most other accused killers. Mitchell's calmness at the prospect of the death penalty impressed even cynical reporters, who appear to have unquestioningly accepted his characterizations of Creffield as a villain and of himself as a virtuous avenger. Consequently, both afternoon newspapers framed the news from Mitchell's perspective, stating flatly that the "fanatic" Creffield had "ruined" women and destroyed families under the false guise of religion. They continued to hold this view, even when the facts did not completely support such an indictment.

Both papers portrayed Mitchell with sympathy, although the *Star* went further than the *Seattle Times,* simply because its coverage was so much more extensive. The *Star* noted Mitchell's "infinite patience" in tracking Creffield, noted his calmness and observed that he demonstrated "not the slightest trace of hesitation or fear of consequences." In a second article that same day, headlined "Revolting Creed of the Holy Rollers," the *Star* quoted George Mitchell at length:

> The tenets of the Holy Rollers were first of all founded upon the theory of free love, which was imposed upon all the membership. His cloak of religion was only a means of getting my innocent sisters into his power. Not warned by the first occasion, when he was tarred and feathered, Creffield got the girls into his power again after he got out of the penitentiary. There was nothing in the world for me to do but to protect the honor of my sisters.

Within a day, reports from Oregon reinforced the sympathetic treatment accorded Mitchell by the *Times* and the *Star.* The *Times* ran a huge headline across the top of its front page:

JUSTIFIABLE HOMICIDE?
IF CORVALIS STORIES ARE TRUE MITCHELL WILL GO FREE!

In bold type just under this headline, the *Times* explained why Mitchell might well go free:

> If the stories from Oregon to the effect that Creffield was the founder of an immoral sect and had been the cause of breaking up many homes, sending many women to the insane asylum and

debauching many young girls, prove true, then Mitchell will be justified for his deed in the eyes of the majority of the people, particularly if his own sisters were involved in the Corvallis orgies.

The *Times* ran another article, also on the May 8 front page, headlined "Mitchell to Get Medal for Murder." The story reported that "a committee of respectable citizens" in Corvallis was planning to present Mitchell "with a handsomely engraved gold medal as a reward for shooting to death Creffield."

In a dramatic move, the *Times* also published an editorial on its front page arguing that—if the stories about Creffield were true—then George Mitchell merited praise, not punishment. The editorial, headlined "SHOULD HE BE PUNISHED?" claimed that only "legal bookworms" would label Creffield's death murder in the first degree. Instead, the paper likened the incident to "the killing of a mad dog," and argued that Mitchell had done the community a great service:

> If this man who was instantly killed on one of the most prominent street corners of the city was the debased brute, clothed in a cloak of religion, he is said to be, George Mitchell deserves immediate freedom that he may display the gold medal his old neighbors in Oregon wish him to wear.[18]

It was a dangerous precedent, the paper allowed, to excuse any and all vengeance for injury done to women, but in this case, Creffield's sordid practices and hypocritical misuse of religion were well beyond the reach of the law—and thus had necessitated Mitchell's drastic action:

> His work was to take a life for the removal of which the law did not provide the means. It was not lynch law—that is usurpation of the functions of the courts. In such cases as this, the courts are powerless. . . . It may not be technically correct to take the life of such a scoundrel—but if there were more men like George Mitchell there would be fewer human beasts and still fewer broken, ruined women in insane asylums and on the streets. . . . If the Oregon stories are true, the issue is plain. The verdict will be largely a matter of public opinion.[19]

In the next few days, newspapers in Oregon—and particularly in Corvallis—rejoiced at the news of Creffield's death. The Corvallis *Gazette* characterized the shooting as evidence of true justice: "Thus do the guilty meet their desserts."[20] The *Gazette* later praised Mitchell:

> In spite of the manner in which the deed was committed, coolly, with premeditation and in defiance of law, there has never been a moment since that everyone familiar with the practices and teachings of the dead Joshua has not affirmed that *Mitchell did a good deed, and was perfectly justified in slaying one who could scarcely be called a human being because of his bestial nature.* This sympathy for the young man who valued his sisters' virtue and fair name above all thoughts of personal safety, and who avenged their ruin to the limit, is universal, and there is hope expressed on all sides that he may be cleared.[21]

The outpouring of support for Mitchell was remarkable. O. V. Hurt said that "Mitchell's well-aimed shot spared others the trouble of sending Creffield to an eternity that he deserved." When the news hit Corvallis, said Hurt, "it spread like wildfire and there was universal joy." Several businessmen in Corvallis sent a telegram to Mitchell, promising to help him, and citizens there began to collect money for a defense fund. The Portland *Oregonian* noted that many believed Creffield "received his just desserts," while Portland's *Oregon Journal* predicted that Mitchell would go free, saying, "whoever is familiar with the creed and practices of the dead man expresses approbation for the deed and regret that the end was postponed so long."[22]

In a highly unusual and widely publicized move, the Multnomah (Portland and vicinity) district attorney, John Manning, not only praised George Mitchell but urged that he escape prosecution. Manning wrote to the King County prosecuting attorney, Kenneth Mackintosh, urging him not to try Mitchell for the murder.

> Creffield broke up many families in Oregon by leading them astray on his fake religion. I investigated many many charges

against him while he was on his Holy Rollering in Oregon, the character of which were perfectly awful, in so far as being low, desperate and brutal, and if permitted, I would like an opportunity to testify before the grand jury, before Mitchell is indicted, or the court, as to the low, degenerate character of this man, and the outrages and brutalities practiced by him, in Oregon, upon ignorant and unsophisticated girls.

Now Mr. MacIntosh, I do not want you to understand that I would not uphold the majesty of the law, but when a man infringes upon the common decency of society to the degree that this man did, and there is no statute under which he could be prosecuted, as he has so grossly debauched families, I think that taking of the law in one's own hands, in such circumstances to mete out summary justice is almost excusable.[23]

The Seattle newspapers were impressed by the sentiment from Oregon, and ran front-page articles with headlines that dwelt on Creffield's remarkable influence[24]—

HOLY ROLLER RULED BY HYPNOTIC POWER

EDMUND CREFFIELD.
Whose Power Over Men and Women Led to His Leadership of the "Holy Rollers" and Eventually to His Tragic Death.

LOUIS SANDELL, OF EAST SE-ATTLE, SAYS CREFFIELD'S EYE MADE WOMEN DO WHATEVER HE WANTED—SISTER IS WITH COLONY IN OREGON WITH HER HUSBAND.

That Edmund Creffield, the "Holy Roller" leader who was shot by George Mitchell, held his sway over women by hypnotic power, is the firm belief of Louis Sandell, of East Seattle. Sandell's sister, Mrs. Frank Hurt, is a member of the sect and is now near Corvallis, where Creffield had planned to unite his followers.

Sandell is very closely connected with all the parties connected in the "Holy Roller" trouble. Frank Hurt, who is the only male member of the "Holy Rollers," married Sandell's younger sister, and it was through his influence that she also became a member of the sect. He also influenced Sandell's other sister, Olive, to go to the "Holy Roller" colony near Corvallis, Ore.

Tried to Save Them.

When Creffield was sent to the

—others that noted Manning's defense of Mitchell[25]—

WHAT AN HONORABLE MAN THINKS OF GEO. MITCHELL

—and still others that detailed the great outpouring of support for Mitchell in Corvallis[26]—

CREFFIELD VICTIM TELLS SAD STORY
CORVALLIS STARTS FUND FOR DEFENSE OF MITCHELL

The *Times* gave a prominent page-one position to an interview with Mitchell's lead defense attorney, Will H. Morris, following the attorney's visit to Oregon. The headline read[27]

CLAIMS MITCHELL RID WORLD OF FIEND

While Mitchell's defenders received substantial coverage in both the *Star* and the *Times* prior to his trial, virtually nothing was written about the local prosecutors or anyone else who did not see Mitchell's actions as justifiable or heroic.

Strong Men Protecting Weak Women

The five-week pretrial crusade by the *Times* and the *Star* to make George Mitchell into a hero succeeded with the public because it resonated so well with contemporary values and beliefs. The first and key ingredient in Mitchell's canonization was the deeply entrenched social belief that men had a duty to defend women. As historian Gail Bederman notes, the early-twentieth-century cult of masculinity—so clearly championed by Teddy Roosevelt and others—emphasized the "natural sex roles" of men and women. In Roosevelt's view, "The man was the armed protector and provider, the woman was the housewife and child-bearer." In 1900, an article in *Cosmopolitan* contended that one component of love was the very dependence of women on men: "That one he loves should look to him for everything—protection, maintenance and happiness—what else can be so thrilling to a manly man?"[28]

The notion that men should protect the moral honor of women was most visible in the South, where "honor" duels and killings long had been the means of redressing sexual improprieties. This notion was also a common defense of violence against Native Americans who were accused of ravishing white women. The very definition of masculinity—among elites as well as lower classes—often meant that men should take pride in attacking other men when that violence was being used to protect women.[29]

The relationship between brothers and sisters was an important part of this code of honor. Sisters were expected to serve their brothers, and brothers in turn were expected to protect their sisters. It was a reciprocal relationship, with duties on both sides.[30] John McGovern's 1883 advice book, *The Golden Censer or the Duties of Today and the Hopes of the Future*, exhorted young men to

> Watch over your sister, to protect her from any association whatever with bad young men, to minister to her wants, to help your parents minister to her health, and to love her with a sincere affection, for as long as you live, you will find her devotion unchangeable, through good and evil report. Look therefore to your sister as perhaps the best friend you will ever have after the death of your mother. Consider her as the person whose interests may be most closely allied with your own than those of any other soul on earth.[31]

Within this context, George Mitchell's claim that "I did only what any true brother would do,"[32] showed him to be a man upholding traditional social values.

Mitchell also found ready sympathy in the Seattle press because his traditional view of the mutual roles of men and women in society was one that resonated well with newspapers in general, and certainly the *Times* and the *Star*. The press was primarily an all-male enclave that viewed women as dependents of men; newspapers throughout the country resisted hiring women at all—except for "society" or "women's news." Both the *Star* and the *Times* routinely reinforced a traditional view of women's roles, responsibilities, and abilities. An editorial in the Seattle *Star* in early 1906 called wifehood and motherhood "the noblest destiny a woman can hope for." Another editorial castigated women who were proponents of divorce, arguing that one of the chief causes of divorce was the fact that women "reformers" had abandoned their home duties to attend political meetings. "They forget that the wife who is always running about to gab fests need feel no surprise if her husband sets up another flat around the corner where someone welcomes him. They forget that the wife whose first business is to make the home all that it ought to be is apt to live in peace and die in the sweet assurance that her husband is faithful." Another editorial expressed the concern that women who worked outside the home ran the risk of losing "the gracious and tender attributes of womanhood." "There is risk of the creation of a third sex—women by nature, but men by environment."[33]

The *Star* ran a contest in May, 1906, asking its male readers to describe their "Ideal Woman." In response, men wrote about women primarily in terms of home and family. One man wrote that his ideal wife was the "angel and idol of home, harmonious companion and counselor" who kept a "good figure" and was also "a good cook and housekeeper." Another wanted a wife who "will always help you to forget your cares and woe and make her presence in your home felt." Another wanted a "good housekeeper, kind to all beings, devoted to family." One man valued "moral display" and "tidiness," while another wanted a wife who was ladylike, with a sweet disposition and who "knows and keeps within her sphere." The ideal woman, it seemed, recognized that her chief role was to be a loyal and loving supporter of husband and children. In return, men had a duty to protect and defend these loyal and helpful women.[34]

The *Times* took a similar approach to gender roles, and its women's pages were filled with news of fashion, women's club meetings, debutante parties, and weddings. A heart-rending short story, run in early May 1906, told of an aging spinster who tragically realizes that she has never known real love. Its advertising columns, like many of that era, give further evidence of the notion of women's weaknesses. An advertisement for Lydia E. Pinkham's Vegetable Compound noted that all women "suffer alike from the same physical disturbance" that led to "the horrors of all kinds of female complaints . . . nervousness, irritability and lassitude."[35]

George Mitchell's story also received a good deal of attention for the simple reason that it was a dramatic, tragic story. Crime has long been big news in the American press, so it was inevitable that the region's newspapers would cover this story in great detail. Public interest in crime had been high from colonial times, when huge crowds gathered for public hangings and publications of execution-day sermons enjoyed high sales. In the early 1830s, when newspapers began to move from strong partisan affiliation toward a more popular, market-driven approach to news, crime became a more prominent and often sensational part of the day's newspapers. The New York *Herald*'s dramatic reporting on the murder of a local prostitute, Helen Jewett, in 1836—replete with detailed and ghoulish descriptions of the bordello and the corpse—demonstrated that the huge public appetite for crime news could greatly increase newspaper circulation and profits.[36] Coverage of crime grew in the following decades, particularly in the late nineteenth century, as intense competition among newspapers put a premium on anything that would increase circulation. Although press attention to crime provoked some criticism, many in the press defended their role, arguing that the best way to deter crime was to hold it up to public scrutiny. For the Seattle press, the Mitchell-Creffield case would provide the basis for a steady stream of sensational stories, and generate demand for many extra editions of the papers.

A Complex Tale

In covering the Mitchell-Creffield case, the *Star* and the *Seattle Times* transformed it from a simple murder into a more complex tale about public order and personal responsibility. By linking the case to broader social concerns of the era, the papers depicted Edmund Creffield as a threat to the American home in general and to women's virtue in particular, and George Mitchell as the defender of both—a dutiful and heroic young man.

The *Star* and the *Times* repeatedly portrayed Creffield as an evil force working against the stability of the home and the nuclear family. "Many of the families of the Corvallis district had been split up when the leader of the sect had made his final appearance," wrote the *Star*. "In many cases, wives left their husbands, daughters forsook their parental roots and among those who became inculcated with the strange belief were Mitchell's two sisters." The *Star* noted that "many of the best homes in the vicinity of Corvallis were ruined," that Creffield was "a notorious religious maniac who had ruined the two sisters of Mitchell and who had broken up homes without number," and that "this man Creffield broke up the Mitchell home in Oregon. He ruined the sisters of George Mitchell and led them astray by his hypocritical teachings and left them in his death mentally weak but still proclaiming them their leader."[37]

The *Seattle Times* repeatedly referred to Creffield as the "destroyer" of homes and quoted at length from a letter written to the paper by an Oregon woman describing her own family's ordeal: "My husband and I have had a loving family broken up and ruined by Creffield, and our sighs and heavy feeling for the ruin he caused in our family was changed to feeling of hope and thankfulness when we heard that the beast was killed." The *Times* also quoted Mitchell's attorney, Will H. Morris, after his return from a so-called fact-finding trip to Oregon, as reporting that Creffield's many women followers had all come from good families, but that those homes had been sundered by Creffield's terrible influence.[38]

In contrast to Creffield, Mitchell was portrayed as the protector of homes. In an editorial, the *Times* characterized the shooting as part of Mitchell's duty to family. "He has merely gone straight at a task which his duty to his family and to the community made him the proper instrument." The paper also quoted one Oregon woman who said that Mitchell, by killing Creffield, had saved numerous lives and homes. As such, Mitchell was no criminal. The *Times* argued that he should be freed from jail on bail, that while confined he was "an associate of criminals and men with whom he has nothing in common." The paper argued further that the law was unjust: "There is not much said on the side of a law which places his act in killing the destroyer of his home alongside the miscreant who shoots down a traveler to rob him of his purse." The *Star* noted that Mitchell had repeatedly pleaded with his sister, Esther, to leave the cult and to return home, and had even sent Esther to live with their father in Illinois in hopes that it would free her from Creffield's power.[39]

Representing Creffield as the destroyer and Mitchell as the protector of homes linked the case to a much larger social debate about the future of the American home, casting Creffield as an opponent of traditional American values and Mitchell as their defender.

The *Star* and the *Seattle Times* also invoked traditional gender roles, arguing that Mitchell was duty-bound to kill Creffield in order to defend the honor of his defenseless sisters. Shortly after the furniture burnings in 1903, the Corvallis *Times* had begun to articulate the notion that Creffield had waylaid "weak" women, and both the *Seattle Times* and the *Star* developed that theme extensively following Creffield's killing. The cult was composed of "defenseless" and "helpless" women, the *Times* reported, while the *Star* stated that only women were susceptible to Creffield's fanatical teaching. Women, by nature the weaker sex, were unable to withstand Creffield's power. Maud Hurt Creffield's father, O. V. Hurt, claimed that Creffield "hypnotized my daughter and she would listen to no one but him." Louis Sandell, whose sister also followed Creffield, said, "I know many of the people he had under his control, and they were perfectly rational and strong minded people before they met him. It was through his hypnotic powers that he got girls under his control. Creffield had a look that seemed to cast a spell over a person and one felt more secure the farther away from him." Sandell claimed that his sister, when rational, understood Creffield's "terrible power" but was unable to withstand him. "I know she was controlled purely by his hypnotism." Such weakness was seen as an inherent condition of women. The *Star* interviewed a psychologist who declared that Creffield could control only those who were predisposed to exploitation. Since the vast majority of those committed to Oregon insane asylums were women, women's inclination to mental instability was clear. Referring to Creffield's followers as "hyperemotional victims," the psychologist argued that "no criminal could influence a moral, conscientiously moral person, for suggestion works successfully along the line of least resistance."[40]

Both newspapers repeatedly wrote of George Mitchell as a hero who had done all he could to rescue his sisters from Creffield's clutches, but who finally concluded that killing him was the only real solution. The *Times* noted that the law had failed to corral Creffield, thus leaving Mitchell little choice. "The old primitive animal law holds, and this was its fulfillment." The *Star* also emphasized the view that Mitchell had really had no choice, quoting Mitchell himself in this regard: "Creffield got the girls into his power again after he got out of the penitentiary. There was nothing in the world for me to do but to protect the honor of my sisters."[41] The *Star* also quoted Louis Sandell, the brother of another young woman who had come under Creffield's sway:

> There was nothing else that Mitchell could do. I saw him in the county jail and he told me he was glad he did the deed, as he would rather suffer in Walla Walla [the state penitentiary] alone than see his whole family ruined forever. As far as the killing is concerned, I know several men who were after Creffield and who would have killed him instantly.[42]

Mitchell's attorney linked the shooting to Mitchell's growing maturity; his client, he said, "had arisen in his manhood and taken the vengeance of nature upon the lustful viper who had stolen the honor of his sisters."[43] Mitchell's maturity was all the more manifest in his calm demeanor. The *Times* reported that Mitchell was unconcerned about his fate, not even asking his attorneys about his chances for acquittal.[44] The *Star* described him as fearless, willing to face whatever punishment given him:

> Mitchell appears well educated and there was nothing of the braggart in his talk. He seemed to take the whole affair as a matter of course and even the officers at police headquarters who observed his every movement closely remarked upon his cool demeanor and entire absence of any fear or excitement. He talked and acted like a sane man who had accomplished a purpose upon which he had been full determined beforehand.[45]

Throughout May and June, both the *Times* and the *Star* portrayed Creffield as a villain and a fiend, and Mitchell as a righteous avenger.

The *Times* referred to Creffield as a "debased brute," a "human beast," the "leader of an immoral sect," a "wretch," and a "fiend" whose "fiendish lust," "deviltry," and "pernicious teaching" ruined women. The *Star* referred to Creffield as a "religious fanatic," the "man who ruined the sisters," a "lawless fanatic," the "destroyer of homes," a "self-styled apostle," a "fanatical leader," a "notorious religious maniac," and a "home wrecker" who "duped" his followers and "led them astray" through "hypocritical teachings." The *Times* referred to Mitchell, in contrast, as a "young man," a "boy who revenged wrongs," a "poor young man," and a "brother who coolly has submitted to the punishment that may await him." The *Star* referred to Mitchell as a "young avenger," a "broken hearted boy" who was "unconcerned and calm" and who gave "a favorable impression."[46]

The two newspapers also relied extensively on news sources and experts who furthered the demonization of Creffield and the canonization of Mitchell—while ignoring sources that might provide a more balanced or even positive view of Creffield. Both provided extensive coverage to Mitchell's attorney upon his return from his fact-finding trip to Oregon. Morris's claim that Mitchell had "rid the world of a fiend" was prominently headlined on the front page of the *Times*. Morris contended that only "half of the wrongs" committed by Creffield could even be described in polite company; the rest were too sordid for words. "It was the unanimous expression of all persons with whom I came in contact," Morris said, "including lawyers, doctors, ministers of the gospel, merchants, peace officers and public officials, that Mitchell's act had relieved the Northwest of the most dangerous brute who ever existed in human form." The *Times* also gave prominent coverage to Morris's highly emotional but vain plea that Mitchell be released on bail:

> I appeal to you as a judge and as a man. I ask you if the slaying of a human leper, killed as you would kill a dog, is a deed to make this man a criminal, to make him a desperate murderer, a man too dangerous to be set at liberty in this community on bail. Can you call this boy, but 23 years of age, a criminal, when he, a green country youth, has arisen in his manhood and taken the

vengeance of nature upon the lustful viper who had stolen the honor of his sisters?[47]

The *Times* noted that the law ruled out bail in a case such as this, but observed that the judge had announced, "If my own feelings were consulted, I admit that my decision might be different, but this is strictly a matter of law."[48]

Other sources included a woman from Cottage Grove, Oregon, who described at length her family's sad breakup because of Creffield, and the superintendent of the Oregon Boys and Girls Aid Society Home, who said that he hoped Mitchell would be "entirely exonerated for ridding the community of a human brute." The brother of one of Creffield's devotees stated that he, too, would have killed Creffield if he had had the chance, and O. V. Hurt—Creffield's father-in-law—declared that Mitchell "has been an instrument in accomplishing a good deed."[49]

The newspapers' prose was often heart-wrenching. The *Star* described "Mothers with babes in their arms were separated from husbands, young girls and single women hardened against fathers and brothers, all as a result of the same false teachings."[50] The letter from the woman in Cottage Grove to the *Times* asked plaintively,

> Would you not, if you were the father or brother of Creffield's victims, kill him like a miserable dog? . . . Put yourself in the place of Mitchell, before he killed Creffield, his young sister ruined, and he the protector. Would you stand the crime against your daughter or sister as long as he did?[51]

The *Star*, ever the champion of the underclass, claimed that the local prosecutor was pursuing the case against Mitchell simply because Mitchell had no powerful friends. The paper recalled that the prosecutor recently had refused to pursue a case against a local man, George Beede, when he shot another man for having paid "attentions" to Beede's wife. "Why is the prosecutor now so eager to hang George Mitchell? . . . And the prosecuting attorney of King County, the man who permitted George Beede to go forth without punishment for a crime equal in intent to that of Mitchell's, says that Mitchell must hang. . . . Why? Mitchell has no influential friends in Seattle, and he may hang for a crime."[52]

Not everyone in Seattle joined the rush to make George Mitchell a hero. Two other local newspapers—the morning *Seattle Post-Intelligencer* and the weekly Seattle *Argus*—avoided the extensive crusading on behalf of Mitchell that so clearly characterized the coverage of the *Star* and the *Times*. The *Post-Intelligencer* provided ample coverage of the case, but engaged in none of the theatrics, flamboyance, or sensationalism that marked the afternoon papers. Part of this reflected the more conservative stance of the *Post-Intelligencer*. The paper was targeted more than the *Times* or *Star* at an upscale audience; as the oldest paper in the city, it also had strong ties to the local Republican political establishment and to Seattle prosecutor Kenneth Mackintosh. The *Post-Intelligencer* covered the key events in the case, noting the shooting and Mitchell's arraignment, but it ran no editorials praising Mitchell, didn't argue (as did the *Star*) in favor of bail for him and ran no articles (as did both the *Star* and the *Times*) reporting that Oregonians wanted to give him a medal. The *Post-Intelligencer* also ignored the press conference held by Mitchell's attorney after his fact-finding trip to Oregon. The paper thus carried little of the more scandalous charges against Creffield, but still allowed its readers to learn about the charges against Creffield and of Mitchell's defense of his actions.

While the *Post-Intelligencer* provided just the key facts in the case, the weekly *Argus*—a Republican paper of opinion and commentary— strongly condemned Creffield's murder, criticized the afternoon newspapers for inflaming public opinion against him, and defended the prosecutor for charging Mitchell with murder. The *Argus*'s editor echoed the prosecutor's arguments, contending that individuals simply could not take the law into their own hands. "Our laws are made to be respected," the paper argued, and "Seattle has had altogether too many murders and attempted murders of the Creffield sort," none of which was really justified. "It is time that the officers of the law let it be understood that they are able to punish criminals without outside interference." The paper accused Seattleites of hypocrisy, saying that they condemned mob lynchings in the South but condoned "one-man murder, on far less provocation, in the North."[53]

The *Argus* also refused to accept Mitchell's argument that he was forced to kill Creffield to uphold the honor of his sisters. It was a "dangerous experiment to allow a murderer or would-be murderer to go free, and then compliment him on his work, merely on his own explanation that the murdered man had done him an unforgivable wrong." In an orderly, lawful society, the courts—not angry individuals—decided the appropriate outcomes. "And yet, for all the public knows to the contrary, he may have simply been a fanatic who should have been locked in an insane asylum."[54] The paper's editor wrote:

There is no excuse for such murders as the one of Creffield in a civilized community, and it will be necessary to hang one or two men like Mitchell, although we may sympathize with them, in order that others may understand that they are not permitted to take the law into their own hands. One may, possibly, be excused in the heat of passion for shooting such a beast down in cold blood. But when a man hunts for another one for weeks, and then sets himself to the task of watching for him, in order to kill him, the element of sudden passion is lacking. Our laws are made to be respected. They are the result of cool and calm deliberation of able minds. Our courts and lawyers are to be depended on to see that they are enforced. When a man is once shot to death his memory stands little chance of being vindicated, no matter if he is wrongfully accused. And for this reason it is a dangerous experiment to allow a murderer or would-be murderer to go free, and then compliment him on his work, merely on his own explanation that the murdered man had done him an unforgivable wrong.[55]

Despite the *Post-Intelligencer*'s more moderate reporting and the *Argus*'s sharp attacks on Mitchell, the afternoon newspapers were successful in creating great support for Mitchell. The combined circulation of the *Star* and the *Times* was more than double the combined circulation of the *Post-Intelligencer* and the *Argus*; moreover, their crusade touched upon social norms that provided a natural reservoir of support for young Mitchell. A widely publicized meeting of the Seattle Chamber of Commerce illustrates this point well. A Seattle banker,

E. Shorrick, introduced a resolution at the chamber condemning the afternoon press for its sensational reporting. "Resolved, that we hereby deplore and condemn the action of the public press in the Mitchell case as tending to encourage the crime of murder as a means of avenging private or family wrongs." The resolution was tabled, however, after other members of the chamber—reflecting the trend in public opinion in town—refused to endorse a resolution that might seem hostile in any way to Mitchell. The president of the chamber, former Governor John H. McGraw, stressed that he had "always stood for the defense of law and order" and repudiated "all forms of lawlessness," but still could imagine cases "where a man's duty to family is paramount." McGraw said that, given the heinousness of Creffield's actions, he doubted he could promise to be an unbiased juror.[56]

As the trial approached, many predicted that Mitchell would be acquitted—that sympathy for the defendant would clearly overcome even Mitchell's own admission that he had killed Creffield with premeditation. A Seattle preacher contended that Mitchell had been "tried by the public and found innocent of murder." As such, he predicted, no jury would convict him. The Corvallis *Times* noted that there were "many who anticipate an acquittal." The Woodburn, Oregon, *Independent* predicted that George Mitchell, if sentenced to be executed, would be pardoned. "If sentenced to a few years in the penitentiary, he may have to serve out the time for ridding the earth of a man who was a fit candidate for the fate meted out to him." Even the *Argus* editor, thoroughly opposed to freeing Mitchell, believed there was a good chance that the local press had so biased the public that a conviction was impossible.[57]

Like the Oregon newspapers earlier in this story, the *Seattle Times* and the *Star* had inflamed public opinion against Creffield through extensive and extravagant coverage. This was a dangerous game, one played in Seattle primarily for circulation gain and with little or no thought to the broader influence or responsibility of the press. Only in the following months, as murder followed murder in Seattle, would editors and reporters begin to realize that the power of the press required a somewhat more measured approach to crime.

While so many strangers rushed to embrace George Mitchell's cause, his own sister—the person he had wanted to save from Creffield's clutches—offered him no support as he awaited trial for murder. Esther believed she had no need for saving, and rather than being grateful, she was implacably angry at her brother and at the many who rushed to portray him as a hero. To her, George was no hero, but rather the man who had destroyed the most compelling person she had ever met. She remained loyal to Creffield, expecting him to rise from the dead and return to lead his followers. She also remained a constant companion to Maud Creffield, and both nursed their grief over Creffield's death, their belief in his resurrection, and, most of all, their hatred of Esther's brother. The Seattle *Star* reported that "practically the first words" Esther uttered upon her arrival in Seattle indicated that she would not help her brother at all. "He had no occasion to do anything to protect me," she said. Esther volunteered to testify against her brother at his trial, saying "I hope my brother will have time to repent of his sins before they hang him."[58]

The *Star* found Esther's behavior inexplicable, for it defied all societal notions of family loyalty and support. The paper saw Esther's denunciation of her brother as nothing less than desertion, and labeled her a traitor:[59]

SISTER TURNS ON MITCHELL

Girl For Whose Honor He Shot Edmund Creffield Says Brother Had No Reason for His Act---Hopes George Will Repent Before He Pays the Penalty.

The *Star* stressed that Esther had "gone back" on her brother "just when he most needs the sympathy of a sister," violating "the great code of blood relationships, known to everyone." The paper noted that she appeared rational most of the time, but not when talking about her brother or Creffield. "Sisterly love has been swept aside by emotionalism of the cruelest and most depraved sort. Honor, self-respect, everything that life holds, she willingly and gladly sacrifices, and calls the whole world to witness the sacrifice."[60]

**WILL HELP CONVICT
HER BROTHER**

ESTHER MITCHELL.

Esther Mitchell's hostility toward her brother defied conventional notions about gender relations, and the press characterized her willingness to testify against George as unnatural. (Seattle Star, 19 May 1906)

5 Defending George Mitchell

If Creffield was guilty of one half of that . . . charged against him,
it would be hard to find a jury anywhere on earth that would convict
his slayer of murder in the first degree.
—SEATTLE *STAR*, JULY 3, 1906

This boy, thrust into the position of the male protector of his sisters,
has done his duty as he saw it.
—*SEATTLE TIMES*, JUNE 28,1906

It was to save his sister from being totally ruined . . . that the young
farmer boy took the law into his own hands and placed himself in
jeopardy because he loved her.
—*SEATTLE TIMES*, JULY 2, 1906

GEORGE MITCHELL'S TRIAL OPENED on Monday, June 25, 1906.
Despite unusually hot weather, the courtroom was packed daily
with reporters and onlookers who were eager to see if the confessed murderer could escape the gallows. Both the Seattle *Star* and
the *Seattle Times* reminded their readers of the gravity of the situation
with identical front-page headlines as the trial opened:

GEORGE MITCHELL ON TRIAL FOR HIS LIFE

Press coverage remained extensive throughout the trial, adding even more to the drama of the case and contributing to the crowds that jammed the courtroom and adjacent hallways. Both the *Seattle Times* and the *Star* covered the trial as though it were a great war, keeping track of each side's successes and failures. They played up emotional testimony and recounted dramatic verbal skirmishes between defense and prosecution. The papers also focused on the growing ranks of women—young and old—who attended court, spoke in whispered tones to Mitchell, and sometimes even brought him flowers. In contrast to his own sister Esther, for whom he had risked so much, these women appreciated his remarkable sacrifice.

The detailed coverage was still highly sympathetic to Mitchell. Throughout the trial, both the *Star* and the *Times* continued to defend Mitchell's actions. The general tenor of their reporting was that Mitchell had done the world a favor by killing Creffield. Driven by overly zealous prosecutors ("legal bookworms," the *Times* called them) and a technicality-laden legal system, society now threatened Mitchell with capital punishment rather than thanking him for ridding the world of a dangerous beast. The *Times* and the *Star* stressed that the "real" people—the people on the street, the people from Oregon who had suffered so much from Creffield—all of these people supported Mitchell. These papers' reports intertwined the "facts" of the case (what occurred in the trial, what witnesses said, etc.) with invocation of social values that implicitly and sometimes explicitly made the case for Mitchell's acquittal. The *Times* and the *Star* were essentially partners with Mitchell's defense attorneys.

The Thaw Case

Just as George Mitchell's trial was starting—on the very first day of jury selection—another sensational "honor" killing occurred across the country, in New York City. This new case did not figure directly in the Mitchell trial, but it gave the Seattle press yet another opportunity to reinforce the notion that men's responsibilities for women—and women's dependence on men—justified extreme actions. In New York, Harry Thaw, a prominent socialite, shot and killed Stanford White, charging that White had "ruined" Thaw's wife. White, a partner in the prestigious New York architectural firm McKim, Mead, and White, was the well-known and widely admired designer of dozens of notable buildings, including the first Madison Square Garden, Madison Square Presbyterian Church, the New York Herald Building, the Washington Square Arch, the Century Club, and residences for some of New York's leading families. Yet he also had a less respectable private life, presiding over lavish, scandalous parties at his apartment in Madison Square Garden.

Among the actresses and starlets who had frequented White's parties was Evelyn Nesbit. After her marriage to the millionaire Thaw, she no longer saw White, but her dubious earlier associations with him inflamed her husband. Just before shooting White in front of hundreds of others at the Madison Square Roof Garden, Thaw shouted, "You've deserved this. You've ruined my home."[1]

Although it would eventually become clear that this case differed greatly from the Mitchell-Creffield case, in its early days it seemed very similar. Newspapers were quick to repeat charges that White had "ruined" not only Thaw's wife but many other young New York showgirls as well. None other than the prominent Victorian crusader Anthony Comstock stated that "If all I have heard about White is true, he deserved his fate." The Seattle *Star*, making clear its views about the case, simplified Comstock's statement in a banner headline on the front page:

"STANFORD WHITE DESERVED HIS FATE"
—ANTHONY COMSTOCK

The *Star* noted that White was a habitué of New York's demimonde, and remarked that his killing disclosed the "greatest sin" in New York City, "the sin of a thousand beautiful girls, weak as they are beautiful, debauched and ruined by men of great minds and wealth . . . who for years have traded on the seeming immunity of their social position and their riches." The *Star* also published an analysis of the Thaw case by an English legal commentator and editor, William T. Stead. Stead avoided condemning or defending Thaw directly, but he argued that murder was quite defensible in certain situations: "Personally, I am quite prepared to justify killing in certain situations. I would like to see all those who prey on female virtue summarily dealt with. Homicide is justified in self defense, in the protection of helpless innocence." The *Star* also carried a front-page illustration of Stanford White's "den of orgies."[2]

The Thaw case, replete with its New York celebrities, eclipsed the Mitchell-Creffield case in newspaper coverage outside of the Pacific Northwest. In Seattle, however, the *Star*'s coverage of the Thaw case served mainly to underscore the heroic view of George Mitchell's actions, invoking notions of endangered women and the heroic men who would sacrifice all to defend them.

The Trial: Selecting a Jury

The opening day of George Mitchell's trial was a microcosm of the entire trial to come, demonstrating the tensions and crosscurrents that would characterize the proceedings right up to their final moments. It immediately became clear that any dispassionate weighing of the facts would be difficult, for the highly opinionated coverage by the *Times* and the *Star* had made it all but impossible to find an unbiased jury. And starting with their earliest questions to the jury, the defense and prosecution set out to steer the trial in completely opposite directions. The *Times* and the *Star* dramatized this struggle, telling readers which side was ostensibly winning the case on any given day.

Heading the defense was Will H. Morris, one of Seattle's leading criminal defense attorneys. Before the Mitchell case, Morris had won acquittals in eleven consecutive first-degree murder cases. He had learned how to craft a case to the best advantage of the defendant, and—perhaps just as importantly—how to browbeat judges and deliver dramatic oratory. Morris's partner, Silas Shipley, was equally adept with the law but less given to dramatic outbursts. Leading the state's case was the county prosecutor, Kenneth Mackintosh, who was known for his formidable legal skills and sharp temper. Assisting him was his chief deputy, John Miller, a former judge who was known for his penetrating mind and remarkable oratorical skills. Presiding over the trial was Superior Court Judge A. W. Frater. Given the huge publicity and the egos of the various attorneys involved, the trial would have been a challenge for any judge. Frater, although well-intentioned, was not particularly adept at controlling the courtroom, and allowed the attorneys to indulge considerably in theatrics and grandstanding.

The first hurdle—finding a jury of twelve men who had not already made up their minds about the case—was a major one, given the sheer volume and nature of reporting on both Creffield and Mitchell by the local press. Almost every prospective juror had heard about the case; of those, many had already formed fairly strong opinions about both Creffield and Mitchell. The *Seattle Times* observed, after the first day of jury selection, that there was "widespread interest in and knowledge of the case, as shown by the fact that all the men examined had read more or less about the case in the newspapers and had, almost without exception, discussed it with others and formed opinions as to the guilt or innocence of the accused."[3]

Dozens of prospective jurors admitted that they had already made up their minds about the case, and Judge Frater excused them from service. James Brackett, from Bothell, confessed under questioning that he had read about the case in the Seattle newspapers and believed that Mitchell should never have been arrested for shooting Creffield. Another prospective juror, a farmer from Vashon Island, said that if what he had read about Creffield in the newspapers was true, then Creffield deserved to be killed. Yet another, Philip N. O'Malley of Seattle, at first indicated that he had no fixed opinion on the case; the prosecution was suspicious of him, however, and after more extensive questioning, O'Malley admitted that he had, indeed, already made up his mind about the case.

Both the prosecution and defense pursued carefully considered—and opposite—strategies. The prosecution sought to keep the trial focused narrowly on the events of May 7, because the case really was about whether Mitchell had murdered Creffield on that day, and because extraneous detail about Creffield's activities would most probably create sympathy among the jury for Mitchell. The defense, in contrast, wanted to focus as much as possible on Creffield, but doing so would prove difficult procedurally.

The defense had few options, given its goal of focusing on Creffield. Both the law and popular culture recognized an "unwritten law" by which sorely aggrieved individuals could take the law into their own hands, but that "unwritten law" usually pertained to fathers defending the honor of their daughters or husbands defending the honor of their wives—not brothers defending sisters. That defense was problematical even for husbands or fathers, however, because many common-law experts simply did not recognize it. By the early twentieth century, a popularized, extralegal notion of the "unwritten law" had, in practice, merged with the defense of temporary insanity as a means of justifying retaliation. In 1904, for example, a Seattle woman, Gertrude Robb, was acquitted for killing George Joye, who had seduced her sixteen-year-old daughter; her attorneys had argued that she was temporarily insane at the time of the shooting. The *Seattle Times* had observed at the time that the temporary-insanity plea "was simply a cloak to get around legal difficulties. The real defense was that a mother has a right to kill a man who ruins her daughter. . . . The written law does not allow persons to settle their personal trouble by taking another's life, but an 'unwritten law' does and this is what saved Mrs. Robb." The temporary-insanity defense allowed Mrs. Robb's lawyers to focus on her state of mind at the time of the shooting, and thus to recount Joye's indecent behavior.[4]

Mitchell's attorneys also used the temporary-insanity defense as a way to focus on Creffield, arguing that the Holy Roller's actions were very much a part of George Mitchell's state of mind at the time of the shooting. Still, this was a difficult strategy given the legal test for insanity in Washington State. The legal test followed the "M'Naghten Rule," which grew out of an 1840s English case. The rule held that "every man is presumed to be sane" until proven insane. The definition of insanity was that the defendant "was labouring under such a defect of reason, from disease of the mind, as not to know the nature and quality of the act he was doing; or if he did know it, that he did not know he was doing what was wrong."[5] In strict legal terms, it would be difficult to show that George Mitchell did not know the nature of his act, given what he had told others before the shooting and during his post-shooting interviews with the police and the media. Indeed, he had readily surrendered to police officers after the shooting and had indicated a willingness to suffer whatever penalty the law demanded.

The first challenge for Mitchell's attorneys was to find jurors who would be willing even to entertain the insanity plea; no matter how sympathetic George Mitchell appeared, jurors who disdained the insanity defense would destroy whatever hope there was for acquittal. Consequently, Morris and Shipley routinely asked several questions of each prospective juror to gauge his views on insanity. One of the questions was, "Have you any prejudice against the defense of insanity in criminal cases, and would you give the same weight to evidence tending to indicate the insanity of an accused person that you would give to evidence of any other character?" In contrast, the prosecution signaled its intent to discount the insanity plea. Prosecutors asked prospective jurors if they would "endeavor to distinguish between the actual insanity of the defendant and a pretense of insanity put up as a means of escaping punishment for a crime."[6]

Conflict soon arose when Judge Frater allowed the prosecution—over the objections of the defense—to follow a line of questioning with jurors that seemed primarily argumentative. The prosecution asked each prospective juror if he believed that a person had the right to take the law into his own hands; defense attorneys believed the questioning was intended to prejudice jurors against Mitchell and objected vociferously, but the judge sided with the prosecution. Emboldened, the prosecutors then asked a question that essentially made the point that Creffield had already been punished for his adulterous behavior by his prison term in 1904–5. Defense attorneys recognized that the prosecution was trying to diminish whatever outrage jurors might feel about Creffield's actions by arguing that he had indeed already been punished for his actions. Again, however, Judge Frater refused to limit the prosecution.[7]

Angered by the prosecution's moves and the judge's acquiescence, defense attorneys escalated their battle with the prosecution, making lurid accusations against Creffield in highly emotional speeches that were only thinly camouflaged as questions. Mitchell's attorneys asked a lengthy question that focused on one of the very central points of the defense—Creffield's involvement with Esther Mitchell:

> If testimony should be introduced in the course of this trial proving, or tending to prove, that the deceased Creffield had so deceived with his teachings the 17 year old unmarried sister

of this defendant, that she fell completely under the sway of his power; if it should be proven that her relatives had caused her to be sent to a reform school for the purpose of getting her out from under his influence; if it should be shown that Creffield, with the aid of this girl's sister, succeeded in getting the girl away from her place of detention and had induced her to run away with him; that he, the said Creffield, had betrayed, seduced and ruined this girl: If it should be shown by the evidence introduced here that immediately before the killing of Creffield by this defendant the said Creffield had prevailed upon this girl he had ruined, to abandon her home and go away to his camp in the mountains, and that the knowledge of this last indignity upon his sister had come to this defendant immediately before the act of killing Creffield; if this evidence is permitted by this court to be introduced for your consideration, will you take it into consideration in making up your verdict in the case?[8]

When the prosecution successfully objected to this question, the defense asked a question of prospective jurors about their attitude towards evidence that would show that mothers had been debauched in the presence of their daughters. The prosecutor again objected, and the judge concurred.

The prosecution's sarcastic rejoinders to defense objections pushed lead defense attorney Morris to even more emotional objections, finally forcing the judge to intervene. He sent the jury pool out of the courtroom and attempted to persuade the attorneys to limit their line of questioning and to avoid the constant fire of objections, arguments, and personal remarks. The defense consistently protested that it was only asking for the latitude enjoyed by the prosecution. Frater's lack of success in controlling the attorneys became clear as the jury pool members filed back into the courtroom. Playing to the jury, Morris remarked that he would fight until hell froze over for justice, and the prosecutor replied, "Let the fireworks go on."[9] They did.

The press described the battles between defense and prosecution in detail, and portrayed the defense as moderately successful in widening the purview of the case. The *Star* observed that the prosecutors were successful in limiting many of the defense's questions, but were

MITCHELL IS AT LAST ON TRIAL

Jury That Will Decide Whether the Killing of Creffield Was Justified

Pervasive and sensational news coverage made jury selection challenging. Both the Times *and* Star *seemed oblivious to the fact that they had contributed to the difficulty.* (Seattle Times, *29 June 1906*)

unable to prevent Morris and Shipley from introducing some of the sensational charges against Creffield. Even when the defense was forbidden from pursuing a certain line of questioning about debauched women, the mere introduction of the question had clearly resonated with prospective jurors. The *Times* observed that, as the defense outlined "the charges of disgraceful orgies" led by Creffield, "the face of more than one honest simple farmer clouded as he listened."[10]

The defense and prosecution attorneys questioned nearly one hundred men—a much larger number than usual for such a trial—before the jury was chosen. The first jury pool of sixty was exhausted by Wednesday, June 27, the third day of the trial. On Thursday, another pool of thirty jurors was called in the county, and deputy sheriffs were dispatched throughout the county to deliver the jury summonses. While the officers were tracking down those summoned, Judge Frater borrowed unneeded prospective jurors from other courtrooms. Finally, at 4:30 on Thursday, June 28—the fourth day of the trial—the defense announced that it was satisfied with the jury and the prosecution concurred. The jurors were sequestered during the trial, staying at a nearby hotel and taking their meals together.

Without acknowledging their own contribution to the difficulty of finding an unbiased jury, the *Times* and the *Star* noted the slow jury selection—calling the process "monotonous" and "tedious." On the trial's third day, the *Star* reported "Slow Work to Pick the Mitchell Jury," while the *Times* ran a headline, "Still Endeavoring to Secure a Jury to Try Mitchell" and commented that the slow pace was "tedious for everyone concerned":

> A penny firecracker would have awakened half the courtroom with a start. Two of the men in the jury box shamelessly slumbered during a good portion of the day. . . . John F. Miller was much interested in the building operations going on outside, which Juror Dore, from an advantageous point near the window seemed to be superintending.[11]

Given the "tedious" nature of jury selection, the *Times* focused extensively on George Mitchell in the early days of the trial. The paper's highly sympathetic coverage continued to link Mitchell to themes of responsibility ("He has done his part"), bravery ("He shows no sign of weakening"), and family loyalty ("to throw his sister out of danger").

> The young man realizes now, if he never did before, that he is on trial for his life. He has done his part. He killed the man who ruined his sisters and broke up their home. . . . The opinions of men have been passed. Most of them have said that Mitchell did right. There now intervenes binding oaths and legal technicalities. . . . Mitchell realizes all of this, but he shows no sign of weakening. . . . In the bottom of his heart, he wishes that this man Creffield had never lived to practice his holy robed deviltries upon his sisters. He wished that they had never come under his spell or at least that he had never heard of them.
>
> But there was nothing about him of the man afraid. It was just the realization of a boy who loves liberty and who loves life that the act which he felt himself compelled to commit has jeopardized them both, that the law has no sentiment, and that he is in the hands of twelve men over whom his lawyers and the attorneys for the prosecution will fight for the next two weeks.

He is like a man who has leaped beneath a swaying rock, hung high on a derrick, to throw his sister out of danger and finds himself prostrate, helpless, able only to wonder whether the rock in its fall will crush him, maim him, or fall to one side. No effort of his can change the result.[12]

In another article, the *Times* romanticized Mitchell's reunion with his father and linked his actions to the act of becoming a man. "The youth has become a man. . . . This boy, thrust into the position of the male protector of his sisters, has done his duty as he saw it." The paper reported that their reunion was a subdued one, for both were quiet people. "It was the silent expression of everything sentimental exemplified by men who have been used all their lives to struggle and fight and sorrow alone, without a sign to the world of the fire of feeling which burns within them."[13]

The *Times* also stressed that Mitchell had many supporters at his trial—people who cared deeply for the young man and who sympathized with his plight. There was a "telepathic current" of support for him in the courtroom, the paper reported. Several women regularly spoke to him to wish him well. "They were not young women or seekers of morbid sensation. They ranged from middle age to white-haired venerability." The *Times* noted that Mitchell was a bit unsure how to react to these very gracious women: "His mother died when he was a small boy, and he is not accustomed to kind words from women who would be sitting beside him if he was their son. He did not know them. He did not even ask their names. They did not give them. He will not even say what they said to him, except that they were very kind." In sharp contrast to these sympathetic women, Esther Mitchell was still "under the baneful influence" of Creffield and unable to recognize her brother's great sacrifice on her behalf. The paper reported that Esther claimed to have had a visitation from God, who excoriated her sister, Donna, for agreeing to testify in George's defense. God, said Esther, "is very angry with her for coming here."[14]

The Trial: The Prosecution

The presentation of the prosecution's case, although not without some disputes from the defense, was the calmest period in the entire trial. In just over one day, the prosecution presented a focused and thorough case against George Mitchell, demonstrating what, indeed, everyone already knew: he had killed Creffield with malice and premeditation. The prosecutors were determined to keep the trial focused on facts relevant to the shooting itself. Both the *Times* and the *Star* portrayed the prosecutors as highly successful in this strategy, and characterized them as regaining the upper hand in the trial. Both papers lamented that the narrow focus was terribly dry and unexciting.

John F. Miller, the deputy prosecuting attorney, outlined the facts of the case in his opening statement on Thursday afternoon. It was a short presentation, and despite his reputation as a powerful orator, he spoke in a low-key manner. He wanted to impress upon the jury how simple and straightforward the case really was. He recounted the key facts: Mitchell "shot and killed Edmund Creffield on the streets of this city." Witnesses would testify that Mitchell had done the deed—and Mitchell himself admitted it. Miller told the jury:

> Officer LeCount came up and found the defendant walking up and down while Mrs. Crefffield scuffled with him, pushing him away from her husband. Someone pointed him out as the man who had fired the shot, but in answer to the policeman's question, he said, "Wait till I get to the police station and I'll make a statement." When he got there he asked for a telegraph blank and sent this message to O.V. Hurt, Corvallis, Oregon: "I've got my man. I am in jail here." That telegram, gentlemen, will be introduced in evidence.[15]

To Louis Sefrit, a *Seattle Times* reporter, he said: "I came here Wednesday morning and had been looking for him. I saw them a block and a half away, and when they passed me I jumped out and fired."[16]

Mitchell listened closely to these opening remarks but displayed no reaction or emotion at all. That would characterize his behavior throughout almost all of the trial; he seemed, one reporter observed, to be merely an onlooker at times, rather than the defendant.[17]

On Friday morning, the prosecution called twelve witnesses to provide the evidence necessary to support the prosecution's case. Dr.

Emil Bories showed the court the bullet that had killed Creffield; he said it had cut through the victim's spinal cord at the second vertebra and had lodged in the right part of his jaw. Creffield died instantly, Bories said. Four men (a jeweler, an insurance agent, a physician, and a bootblack) who had heard the shot and rushed to the scene also testified. They all told the same story: they heard the report of the gun, hurried to the scene, and saw Mrs. Creffield hitting Mitchell. Two of these witnesses noted that Mitchell was very calm.[18]

Other prosecution witnesses also stressed that Mitchell was calm after the shooting. One police officer, LeCount, said that Mitchell "was cool and collected and showed no evidence of agitation." Charles Tennant, a Seattle police detective who booked Mitchell, said the defendant was "cool and calm" at the jail. The police chief, Charles Wappenstein, recounted that he had cautioned Mitchell against giving interviews to reporters because the information could be used against him in court, but Mitchell had insisted that he was unafraid. Louis Sefrit, the *Times* reporter, testified that Mitchell very calmly explained his motives, indicating that he had shot Creffield because the man had "ruined" his two sisters. Sefrit testified that Mitchell told him that he "had only done his duty."[19]

The most dramatic part of the prosecution's case was the testimony of Creffield's widow, Maud. The *Times* described the entrance of Creffield's widow in the courtroom and suggested that she was still in the thrall of Creffieldism:

Standing in the midst of the crowded courtroom, neatly gowned all in black, her eyes blazing with the fire which seems to burn in the look of every one of the women who believed and still believe that Franz Edmund Creffield was in truth Joshua returned to life, Mrs. Maud Creffield, his widow, appeared for a dramatic moment this morning. . . .

There was an intentness in her demeanor which was almost defiance. Whatever it was in her—religious fervor, fanatic belief that her husband still lived, spiritualistic confidence, hate for the man who had slain her husband or a sense of martyrdom—gave her an expression and a bearing different from any ordinary woman.

Her appearance was startling. It sent a thrill which was almost a shiver through the men inside the rail who turned in their chairs to meet that blazing look in her eyes.[20]

Under questioning, Maud identified Mitchell as the man who had shot her husband, but she soon became distraught and nearly fainted on the stand. She surprised everyone in the courtroom by indicating that Mitchell had spoken to her after the shooting; none of the other witnesses had heard him speak to her. The entire courtroom became silent as Miller asked her what Mitchell had said. She was unable to reply, however; twice she opened her mouth as if to speak, but both times she was unable to do so. Miller did not push her on this point. He did ask her, however, to show how she had seized Mitchell by the arms after the shooting. She stood to do so, but immediately began to sink to her knees. With that, Miller ended his questions.[21]

Throughout the presentation of their case, the prosecutors focused exclusively on the events of May 7—on the shooting itself and its immediate aftermath. They made no reference to earlier events, thus making the history of Creffield an irrelevant and inappropriate subject for cross-examination by the defense. The defense tried anyway, but prosecutors were quick to object—and the judge was just as quick to side with the prosecution. Still the defense tried, hoping for a slip somewhere. Morris's cross-examination of Maud Creffield was fairly lenient; by the time he questioned her she was on the verge of a complete collapse. Still, Morris tried to get her to talk about her two marriages to Creffield, thus introducing a complication that would need some explanation—which would, in turn, allow for questions that focused on the history of Creffield and the cult. They also tried to get her to talk about the cult generally, and about Creffield's assumption of the name "Joshua." With rapid-fire objections, the prosecution succeeded in having all of these questions rejected, but the defense persisted. At one point, Judge Frater—at the prosecution's behest—warned defense attorneys not to ask questions they knew would be disallowed merely to plant ideas in the heads of jurors. After a string of rulings against them, the defense attorneys began to argue so vociferously against the judge's rulings that Judge Frater had the jury removed from the courtroom. Defense attorney Morris contended that it was the "duty of the sworn officers of the law" not only to prosecute but also "to present all of the facts for consideration"—meaning a broader review of Creffield's checkered career. Despite that claim and other arguments from the defense, Frater stood firm.[22]

Both the *Times* and the *Star* noted the prosecution's skill in presenting its case; in the newspapers' view, the prosecution clearly had the edge over the defense in the opening days of the trial. The *Times* detailed the "calmness and coldness" of the facts as the prosecution presented them, saying that the prosecution "has sought to impress the jury with the simplicity of its case and thereby with the fact that nothing can mitigate its array of frigid facts indicating meditated murder." The *Star* noted that the defense had so far failed to make its case that Mitchell had acted honorably. Unless the defense had greater success soon, the *Star* observed, the trial would be quite short.[23]

Both papers seemed disappointed by the calm manner of the prosecution; the *Times* said the trial had been "prosaic" so far, and the *Star* characterized the prosecution's case as "a simple and formal one, almost to the point of being devoid of unusual interest." The papers seemed to be looking forward to the opening of the defense, promising their readers that the excitement level of the trial would soon increase. The *Star* told its readers that "the real interesting features of the trial will begin" with the defense. The *Times* advised that

> Tomorrow the fireworks will begin, for just as the prosecution attempts to curb any natural tendencies toward emotion upon the part of the jury, the defense aims to encourage it. The defense claims to have an argument just as logical and just as legal as the statements of fact presented by the prosecution, but their case concerns the emotion of a man and that of the [prosecution] the dry facts of law books.[24]

The Trial: The Defense

As predicted by both the *Times* and the *Star,* the defense portion of the trial was indeed far more dramatic than the prosecution. That drama derived from the defense's valiant—and ultimately successful—efforts to put Creffield's character on trial, and from the compelling and tragic testimony given by Mitchell's supporters. The drama also derived from the coverage by the *Times* and the *Star,* which continued to portray Mitchell sympathetically and which began to report that the defense was winning the trial.

On the day the defense began its case, the *Star*'s page-one story focused on the wide support that the defendant had. A large four-column headline proclaimed:[25]

"GOD BLESS YOU, GEORGE; WE'RE PRAYING FOR YOU"

Slayer of Creffield Is Loaded With Flowers as He Marches From Prisoner's Dock to Cell --Defense Outlines What Will be Used to Prove That Mitchell Was Insane at Time of the Killing.

The article told the story of women—some young, others in their sixties and seventies— who greeted Mitchell affectionately at the trial every day. Some brought flowers, others just shed tears at his ordeal. The *Star* noted Mitchell's quiet gratitude for the support. "Two or three times he tried to express himself in words, but that lump in his throat seemed always in the way, and he hurried on so that those who interrupted his walk to prison should not see the moisture in his eyes." Although the *Star* did not mention Esther Mitchell, the contrast between these women and her stony refusal to support him was vivid. The *Star*'s article also stressed the "facts" of the defense's case—that Creffield had "ruined" Mitchell's sisters and that his "baneful influence" lingered still.[26]

The *Times,* which had already run an article on Mitchell's supporters, discussed the difficult task ahead for the defense. The most logical witnesses for the defense—the witnesses who could best testify to the activities of Creffield and his followers—were still "under the spell" of the Holy Roller and consequently hostile to the defense. Mitchell's attorneys thus ran into "a wall of fanatical mysticism" in their effort to save his life. Lest anyone forget, the *Times* also repeated the implicit charges against Creffield: he had a baneful influence over his followers and had split up families.[27]

As much as the prosecution had been brief, the defense was not. Mitchell's attorneys had much to do. They needed, first, to provide evidence that Mitchell was insane at the time he shot Creffield; that would be hard to do, particularly given his calm demeanor, his ready admission of guilt immediately after Creffield's death, and the fact that he had never been hospitalized or treated for any kind of emotional distress. Second, they needed to shift the focus away from the events of May 7 to the history from Corvallis and Portland. Given the actual charges against Mitchell, the narrow focus of the prosecution, and the judge's strict rulings on what constituted relevant evidence, that, too, would be difficult. Both defense attorneys—and particularly the showboating Morris—thrived on difficult cases, and they planned an aggressive defense with more than two dozen witnesses.

Silas Shipley made the opening statements for the defense, speaking for nearly four hours (compared to a mere ten minutes for the prosecution's opening statement). Attorneys have a good deal of latitude in these opening statements, as they outline what they intend to prove through sworn testimony. Shipley made the best of the moment, outlining the sordid history of Edmund Creffield (whom he usually called "Joshua" in order to emphasize Creffield's religious delusions) and his influence over his followers and particularly over Esther Mitchell. Shipley told of the Holy Rollers' tumultuous rituals, of Creffield's tar and feathering, of his conviction for seducing George Mitchell's sister, Donna Starr, and of the efforts by numerous Corvallis men to kill Creffield in the spring of 1906.

The most interesting part of Shipley's opening statement was his discussion of Mitchell's mental state at the time of the shooting. For the first time, Mitchell was portrayed as a seriously unbalanced young man with severe religious delusions. Shipley argued that Mitchell, "in taking the life of Joshua Creffield on the morning of May 7, believed that he was performing an act for which he had been especially selected by God." According to the defense, Mitchell believed that his dead mother had appeared to him, telling him that God wanted him to kill Creffield. Shipley claimed that Mitchell had told several people

Attorneys for the Defense
In Mitchell Murder Trial
Calvert
MESSRS. MORRIS (at the right) AND SHIPLEY, SKETCHED BY CALVERT

*Mitchell's attorneys, Silas Shipley and Will Morris, did much to help the press and the jury to focus the case not on Mitchell's crime but on Creffield's dubious practices. (*Seattle Times, *28 June 1906)*

of his divine mission: "I am the only one who can kill Creffield, and I am going to do it. God has revealed to me a command that I should go and get him and deliver him over to God."[28]

Shipley maintained that Mitchell's obvious calmness after the shooting—which had been so remarked upon by the prosecution and its witnesses—was simply a manifestation of the full degree of his delusion that he was not bound by the laws of man. Invoking then-contemporary beliefs about insanity, Shipley argued that Mitchell's afflictions were hereditary in nature, manifested by his father's mono-mania for religion and his two sisters' obviously insane loyalty to Cref-field. Shipley told the jury that the defense would indulge in no "pettifogging"; the case was simple: "While not denying that it was the defendant's hand that fired the shot, we do deny that his act at that time was controlled by a mind in the possession of its rational and reasoning faculties to such an extent as to apprehend the true relation which he bore to his surroundings and responsibilities and obligations he rested under to others or to realize the true nature of the act."[29]

This representation of Mitchell was a novel one, and certainly at odds with how he himself had represented his actions shortly after the killing. He had made no mention of conversations with his dead mother or of a divine task. Instead, he had frankly admitted that he shot Creffield because he believed the religious leader had "ruined" his sisters. He had seemed quite aware of violating the law, indicating that he was willing to take whatever punishment he faced. None of Mitchell's friends or supporters in Oregon reported hearing of such religious delusions, either, even though some—such as O. V. Hurt—had remained in fairly constant contact with young Mitchell. Even the *Seattle Times*—which had been so lavish in its support for Mitchell since the shooting—commented that "some of the statements made by Mr. Shipley were of such a nature as to tax one's powers of belief in their possibility."[30]

The witness who had caused the most sensation before the start of the trial—Esther Mitchell—appeared immediately after the defense's opening statement. This was the first time that Esther and George had seen one another since Creffield's death, and it was a moment that clearly captured the tremendous gulf between them. George looked nervous throughout Esther's testimony, continually folding and unfolding his hands and biting his lips. Esther, in contrast, was cold and distant, a very reluctant witness who gave minimal answers to the questions from defense attorneys. Morris and Shipley apparently did not expect much from Esther, and did not press her in questioning. Esther refused to acknowledge George in any way, and her coldness also extended to their brother Perry, who supported George and sat with him at the defense table. When Perry Mitchell saw Esther in the courthouse hallway, he attempted to talk to her. She was willing to shake his hand but refused any further conversation, simply saying "Stand aside, please." Their sister Donna, who had originally come to Seattle to testify on George's behalf, had changed her mind after talking to Esther. She even refused to come to court, and a bench warrant was issued and deputies dispatched to escort her to the courtroom. On the stand, she—like Esther—was an unwilling and "sullen" witness. Donna, the *Times* reported, "would do nothing she was not compelled to do by the law to lend aid to her brother."[31]

The *Times* stressed that Esther's natural attitude should have been one of gratitude and support for her brother. The paper commented, "She is one of the few persons on earth whom the naturally prevailing rule of blood kinship should bring to his side, almost with perjury if that were necessary." Lamenting "that the sister has no appreciation of this great love in which she is held by her brother and decries his act in taking the life of the man who would have destroyed her," the *Times* characterized her as a "child, who deadened of all love for family, would see her brother punished for what he has done in her behalf." It also noted that only a "brief conversation" with Esther had revived Donna's "prejudices of religious fantasy" and that she, too, had now turned against her brother.[32]

For the *Times*, this hostility from both Esther and Donna seemed only to underscore the extreme emotional instability of women. The paper noted that women were far more likely than men to fall under such an influence; men were usually repelled by "the more unusual of the demonstrative elements of religion." These women were mentally weak, the paper declared:

> These witnesses . . . are not mental heavyweights. They are simple folks. In their minds it is not easy to distinguish between religious doctrine which is good and sound and uplifting, and a frenzy, based upon the same fundamental idea—the pleasing of God—which more cultivated minds immediately pronounce evil, degrading and bestial.[33]

The *Times* described Esther as behaving primarily as "an automaton," and characterized the two sisters, Esther and Donna, as "peculiar looking women" with "a strange look in their eyes." In contrast, George

Mitchell was, despite the defense's insanity argument, still depicted by the *Times* as a paragon of emotional stability, a young man cognizant of his responsibilities to family. The paper trumpeted his great love for Esther, saying he acted "to save his sister from being totally ruined by the man who held her in the hollow of his hand."[34]

The testimony of George Mitchell's sisters did little to advance the defense's case. Like some of the other witnesses they would call later in the trial, the purpose in calling them may well have been more emotional than legal in nature; the defense attorneys wanted the jury to see the women still under the thrall of the slain cult leader. The next major witness, however, was probably the most important one of the entire trial.

On July 3, 1906, O. V. Hurt—father of Maud Creffield, father-in-law to the slain Creffield—was called to the stand and recounted in detail the tragic history of Creffieldism in Corvallis. Hurt's testimony succeeded in focusing the case squarely on Edmund Creffield. Members of the prosecutor's staff would later concede that they believed that any hope they had of convicting Mitchell evaporated with Hurt's testimony. These insiders said that Mackintosh and Miller believed that the defense could have rested without a single additional witness and won an acquittal.

The *Star*'s headlines summed up Hurt's testimony well:

HURT TELLS THE HORRIBLE STORY OF HOLY ROLLERISM

With Tears in His Eyes Corvallis Man Recounts the Wrongs Committed by Creffield---Dramatic Testimony of Ruined Home, Debauched Wife and Debased Sisters.

Based on Hurt's testimony, the *Star* observed, "If Creffield was guilty of one-half of that which Hurt charges against him, it would be hard to find a jury anywhere on earth that would convict his slayer of murder in the first degree."[35]

The *Times* also played up the great drama of Hurt's testimony and emphasized his indictment of Creffield:

TELLS HOW RUIN CAME TO HIS FAMILY

O.V. HURT, PRINCIPAL WITNESS IN MITCHELL TRIAL, WEEPS AS HE GOES INTO DETAILS OF JOSHUA'S REIGN

In its article, the *Times* described Hurt's testimony as "the halting story of a man who has seen his loved ones fall victims to the spell cast by a lustful human who accomplished his desires only after he has convinced those he ruined that he was God." It observed that Hurt found the testimony painful, but "he felt that in so doing he was helping to save from the unsympathetic hand of the law the man who avenging his own wrongs had revenged the wrongs of others." The *Times*'s reporter also stressed the drama of the testimony:

> Neither did any forensic display accompany this story of ruined lives, but it was tragedy nevertheless for a strong man nerved himself to place before the public the remnants of a broken heart; to tell to all the world the details of that which had caused him grief and shame greater than which no man can know.[36]

Hurt was an impressive witness. Middle-aged, a respectable merchant and political leader, he had endured the full gamut of Creffieldism. Creffield's earliest devotees had met in Hurt's home; there they had set their first bonfires and destroyed gardens and sidewalks. Hurt's own daughter, Maud, had married Creffield. Esther Mitchell had lived in his home, and he treated young George Mitchell like a son.

Sobbing at times and near emotional collapse, Hurt described in painful detail Creffield's history in Corvallis: the tumultuous rituals; bonfires that destroyed furniture, cats, and dogs; the alienation of his wife; Creffield's hiding under the Hurt home; the "ruin" and asylum commitment of his wife and daughter; and on and on. "That man, gentlemen of the jury, ruined my life. He ruined my home and my family." Hurt also testified that he had told George Mitchell that Creffield had "ruined his sisters." Mitchell, said Hurt, was acting "a crazy man," claiming to have a message from the spirits to kill Creffield.[37]

Prosecutors attempted to derail Hurt's testimony, arguing repeatedly that many of the details were simply not relevant. Judge Frater did exclude some of the testimony, but the sum and substance provided a shocking indictment of Creffield. Moreover, as the Portland *Oregonian* reported, "several of the jurors displayed marked irritation at the frequent interruptions of the state, with its objections to statements offered by Mr. Hurt in evidence." Their interest is no surprise, given the drama of Hurt's testimony. On several occasions, he had to pause, obviously fighting for self-control. When he described the ravings of his wife and of "my little daughter," his deep sorrow was palpable. At one point, his quiet sobbing echoed through the hushed courtroom. The *Oregonian* observed that "the jury and courtroom were moved by what they heard."[38]

After Hurt, the defense called Burgess (Burt) E. Starr—the husband of Donna Starr, George Mitchell's sister. Starr told of his wife's efforts, under Creffield's direction, to free Esther from the Boys and Girls Aid Society Home in Portland. He disclosed his wife's adultery with Creffield and her rolling on the floor of their home in a kind of religious trance. Sobbing, he also described how Donna had deserted him and their three young children to follow Creffield to his wind-swept camp on the Oregon coast, stealing away in the middle of the night to avoid her children's cries. George Mitchell had visited the Starr household shortly after Donna's flight, and Starr had showed him her short farewell note, which read:

> I cannot wait until daylight because the babies will cry to go with me. I have taken about $2.50 of your money, but I guess I have been worth that much to you. It is not enough to pay my fare and I will have to walk to the place I am going.

As Starr recounted, "George took my little ones on his knees and wept while he caressed them and told them that he would go and bring their mother back."[39]

In its coverage, the *Times* emphasized not Starr's testimony but Mitchell's reactions to it. The paper reiterated Mitchell's great concern for his sister and reminded readers that he had taken on a man's role as protector of his family—even though he was so young ("a farmer boy") that unmanly emotions still surfaced occasionally. The contrast between Mitchell and his brother-in-law Burt Starr was vivid, too: whereas Starr had seemed helpless after his wife deserted him and his children, Mitchell had resolutely set out to return his sister to her family.

MITCHELL WEEPS WHILE STARR TESTIFIES

For First Time Since His
Arrest Slayer of Creffield
Allows Feelings to Get Better
of His Self-Restraint

Story of His Parting From
Sister's Little Ones Before
Starting Out to Hunt Joshua
Unmans Him for Moment

For the first time since he was placed on trial for the killing of Joshua Creffield, George Mitchell yesterday afternoon permitted his emotions to gain ascendancy over the stoicism which has marked his demeanor ever since his arrest. . . . This farmer boy has been under that terrible strain of hearing the story of his sisters' disgrace unfolded to a carping public and although the leash in which he has bound his feelings has tightened to the breaking point time and again it held true until this moment.

It was the sobbed out story of Burgess Starr, Mitchell's brother-in-law, which broke down the barrier of self-repression the latter has maintained throughout the weary days he has spent in court. . . . Before there had been tears in Mitchell's eyes but now he laid his head on his arms and his shoulders shook with sobs. It was only for a moment, however, and then the boy straightened up and from that time on gave no evidence that the proceedings held even a passing interest for him.[40]

Both the *Seattle Times* and the *Star* continued to comment on Mitchell's many supporters. The *Times* also noted a mysterious woman—"well dressed and good to look upon"—who was a constant observer at the trial and who regularly brought Mitchell roses. Who was this mystery woman? She refused to give her name, but Mitchell was clearly fond of her. He wore one of her roses in his coat lapel "and occasionally during the day turns around to give and receive a smile of recognition." But when O. V. Hurt brought flowers to Mitchell, Judge Frater finally had had enough, and ruled that no one could give flowers to the defendant while jurors were present.[41]

Jurors continued to see the many well-wishers who approached Mitchell each day, however. Many of those attending the trial were from Portland; they greeted the young man each day as he was escorted by deputies from his jail cell to the courtroom. In the early days of the trial, the courtroom was packed, with every inch of standing room taken and an officer stationed at the courtroom door to keep others outside. Eventually, the judge had enough of the crowds as well, and limited attendance to those who could find seats. Because seating was limited, many courtroom observers stayed in the courthouse or close by during the lunch hour, so that they could quickly reclaim a seat when the trial resumed in the afternoon.[42]

Another of Mitchell's supporters was John Manning, the district attorney from Portland (Multnomah County). Manning had urged Seattle prosecutors not to charge Mitchell with a crime, and he came to Seattle to testify for the defense. The *Seattle Times* sent a reporter to interview Manning at his hotel, and in a front-page story printed Manning's claims that Oregonians would have thanked Mitchell rather than prosecuted him for killing Creffield. "No court in the state of Oregon would ever have convicted Creffield's slayer of any criminal act in removing such a beast from the face of the earth," Manning said, "There is no possibility that Mitchell or any other man who would have had the nerve to put Creffield out of the way would have ever had to suffer any penalty for an act that would only have been considered in the light of a public benefit." The *Times* reported that the details of Manning's testimony "are too shocking for publication," and predicted he would provide dramatic and substantive support for Mitchell's defense—if the prosecution did not block him from taking the stand.[43]

The prosecution did, in fact, prevent Manning from testifying, on the basis that his testimony was not directly relevant to the charges against Mitchell. Nonetheless, Manning's brief appearance in the courtroom was notable; as the Portland *Oregonian* reported, "The court-room was crowded with spectators anxious to behold the somewhat unusual sight of a public prosecutor appearing in the interests of a man accused of murder." Just in case anyone had missed the point that he supported Mitchell, the Oregon prosecutor had walked over to the table where the defendant was sitting and—in front of the jury—"shook him heartily by the hand and told him to keep a stiff upper lip, as he would come out all right in the end."[44]

Other witnesses from Oregon provided further testimony regarding George's great sorrow over Esther Mitchell's devotion to Creffield. Two officials from the Boys and Girls Aid Society Home in Portland testified that George wanted to protect Esther from Creffield's influence; they also said that Esther's emotional turmoil deeply grieved her brother. At one point, William D. Gardner said, George refused to even see his sister during one of her religious rantings, saying, "No, I cannot stand to see her. I never want to see her while she is in that condition."[45]

In the latter days of the trial, the Seattle press recounted the testimony from other Oregonians who said that they also had wanted to kill Creffield:[46]

WANTED A CHANCE TO KILL CREFFIELD

AGED WITNESS TESTIFIED THAT HE ASKED MITCHELL TO BE ALLOWED TO SLAY HOLY ROLLER LEADER — TRIAL IS NOW AN EMPTY FORM

and others who were convinced that George was temporarily insane:[47]

ARE SURE MITCHELL WAS OUT OF HIS MIND

Corvallis residents who had publicly praised Mitchell shortly after the shooting now told stories not about his heroism but about his mental instability, to fit the defense's strategy. They invariably reinforced the image of Mitchell as a highly responsible young man who was deeply dedicated to his sisters. Two Corvallis residents who had tried to kill Creffield recounted how they told Mitchell of the destruction Creffield had brought to their families. Louis Hartley told the jury, "My object, gentlemen, to be frank with you, was to kill Creffield." Repeating a now familiar refrain, Hartley said that Creffield "ruined my family." D. H. Baldwin, also of Corvallis, testified that he had forcibly removed his "weak and emaciated" daughter from Creffield's camp, and then had vowed to kill Creffield to prevent him from ever controlling his daughter again. Baldwin also testified that he had told Mitchell all of this only shortly before Creffield's killing. Baldwin asserted that he believed that Mitchell was insane when he saw him on May 1 at the Corvallis railroad station; prosecutors tried to shake his testimony but he would not budge. Baldwin said he had argued with Mitchell, pointing out that Mitchell was much younger than he—"with his life ahead of him and with every opportunity offered to upright young men. The better days of his life were still to come." Baldwin said that he, as a much older man, had but a few years left to live and thus was the appropriate agent to kill Creffield, because whatever punishment Baldwin would face would be inconsequential given that his life was nearly over. The *Star* told its readers that the testimony of Baldwin and Hartley had touched the hearts of the jurors.[48]

Even before the trial concluded, both the *Seattle Times* and the *Star* began to predict that Mitchell would be acquitted. On July 5, the *Star* announced that the trial was essentially over. Everyone in the courtroom, including the prosecution, the *Star* reported, knew that the jury would vote to acquit. Whether Mitchell was insane or not did not matter; he removed "a pestilence whose blighting influence has wrecked homes and broken hearts, ruined women and driven strong men to despair. *That's all there is to the Mitchell case.*"[49]

Sane or insane—laboring under what he believed to be a God-given command or in full possession of all of his mental powers when he committed the deed, there seems to be everywhere, even at the table of the prosecuting attorneys, a feeling that it is all a farce—that all the wrangling and bickering about the introduction of that or this bit of evidence is purely a waste of time and energy—that the 12 good men and true who sit in the jury box, if they don't believe George Mitchell to be insane, are going to perjure themselves—it's a strong word, but it fits—in order to free the boy who sits through the warm hours of the trial and waits until that verdict comes.

The trial will drag along for another week perhaps. The jury will eat and sleep and listen. The lawyers will mop their brows and talk and wrangle just as though it was all for some purpose. The honorable court will play his role in the farce, will sustain and overrule objections, will warn the curious people who come to listen that if they laugh aloud again he'll put them out, and will go on silently chewing gum. And then will come the verdict and if it's other than acquittal, it will be the biggest surprise that ever came from Profanity hill. And up from Oregon there'll come a roar of anguish that will continue to echo and re-echo until succeeding generations will have forgotten all about the story of the Holy Rollers and their degenerate leader.[50]

On the next day, the *Star* continued in this vein, noting that there had been several witnesses on the stand but that virtually nothing had occurred of any major consequence. The paper's front-page story focused on two things: first, a "tall woman with a big voice" who accused the deputy prosecutor of trying to get rich by prosecuting "poor George Mitchell," and second, the absence of the mysterious woman who brought flowers to the accused. "Mitchell seemed to miss her, too, for he looked about as he rose from his seat at the noon recess and a shade of disappointment crossed his face." The jurors had made up their minds, the *Star* said: they were tired and wanted to go home to their families. The paper also noted that the prosecution's many objections were unable to deflect the defense's arguments; Mitchell's attorneys "are making all of the case that the material at their hands will permit."[51]

The *Times* reported on July 7, 1906, that the defense attorneys had won a great victory when they were able to put insanity experts on the stand.

SIGNAL VICTORY FOR MITCHELL DEFENSE

FOR FIRST TIME ATTORNEYS FOR SLAYER OF CREFFIELD SUCCEED IN GETTING EXPERT INSANITY TESTIMONY BEFORE JURY

The most significant mental-health testimony came from Dr. John Nicholson, an expert in nervous diseases and a former physician at the Minnesota state insane asylum. In response to hypothetical questions, Nicholson stated that anyone acting as Mitchell had done would clearly be insane at the time of the shooting. Nicholson also testified that insanity was often hereditary and that the mental imbalance of one sibling was often indicative of similar problems in another sibling. Nicholson was a knowledgeable witness, and the prosecution was unable to shake his testimony.[52]

The next day, the *Times* reported that attorneys who had listened to the proceedings believed that the defense would win; the *Star* predicted that the jury would need little time to reach a not-guilty verdict. The *Star* also reported that prosecutors realized that there was no hope for a first-degree murder conviction; they were just hoping for any verdict other than acquittal.[53]

The Trial: Closing Arguments

Even though the *Star* and the *Times* pronounced the case over, there was still more drama to come in the courtroom. Shortly after they finished their defense, George Mitchell's attorneys offered to submit the case to the jury without closing arguments. Their goal was to prevent the prosecution—particularly John Miller, a highly persuasive speaker—from focusing the case anew on Mitchell instead of Creffield. Prosecutors were outraged, but feared antagonizing a palpably exhausted jury. Still, prosecutors insisted on their right to make closing arguments, telling the judge and jury that the law provided for such arguments and that they would be shirking their duty if they quit too soon. The judge concurred with the prosecution. The defense then countered, arguing for a two-hour time limit on closing arguments—but the prosecutors again objected and the judge again concurred with them.

The prosecution had District Attorney Mackintosh speak first, to remind the jury of the clear-cut facts in the case and to assail the insanity plea. He spoke for just twenty minutes, arguing that Mitchell was clearly guilty of first-degree murder and that the insanity defense was really the resort of those who had no defense at all. Citing a Washington State supreme court case, Mackintosh told the jury, "The world has had quite enough of that kind of insanity that begins just as the sight of the slayer, ranging along the barrel of a pistol, marks a mortal spot on the body of the victim, and ends as soon as the bullet has sped on its final mission."[54]

When Mackintosh finished his general overview of the case, Morris and Shipley told the judge and jury that the defense would waive its right to argument, thus ending closing arguments and preventing Miller from addressing the jury. The judge and prosecutors were stunned, and the judge quickly sent the jury out of the courtroom while he tried to figure out how to proceed. At first, Frater indicated that he would allow the defense's ploy, but after a lunch break he ruled that the prosecution could make further closing remarks. The prosecutors reluctantly decided not to do so, fearing they would alienate the jury by prolonging the case. Frater then gave brief instructions to the jury, stressing that jurors could only acquit Mitchell if they accepted the insanity defense. He also told the jurors that a manslaughter verdict would not be accepted; if guilty at all, the defendant was guilty of first- or second-degree murder.[55]

The jurors filed out of the courtroom at 3:14 P.M. Most of the participants and observers of the trial remained in the courtroom, expecting that a verdict might come quickly. They were not disappointed. After less than ninety minutes, the jurors signaled that they had a verdict. At 4:45 P.M., Frater ordered the jury brought into the courtroom; he then cautioned everyone in the courtroom that he would tolerate no demonstrations, whatever the verdict. Everyone was tense. As the *Seattle Post-Intelligencer* reported, "The audience listened with bated breath to the proceedings of the court, the polling of the jury, the question by the judge and the handing of the verdict to the judge." The *Star* recounted what happened next:

When the words "not guilty" were reached, the crowd, disregarding the court's previous instructions, broke into cheers and handclapping. Then began the handshaking and the congratulations. . . . Men and women crowded about the man who had just been freed from the charge of murder.

The bailiff pounded his gavel to silence the din, and an angry Judge Frater told the sheriff to take custody of Mitchell. Mitchell's attorney William Morris objected, noting that he had been found not guilty. Morris told the judge, "This man is innocent, and I want him to be free. If you are going to give him into the custody of the sheriff, I want to begin habeas corpus immediately." Frater stated he merely wanted to clear the courtroom and wanted him taken back to the jail, but Morris again objected heatedly. At that point Frater gave in, ordering the sheriff to release Mitchell.[56]

Mitchell briefly returned to the jail to retrieve his few possessions, and then headed out into the city streets with his brother, attorneys, and friends. Pausing in front of the courthouse, Mitchell thanked his attorneys, the jurors, and particularly the Oregonians who had supported him. "I am particularly thankful that the people of Oregon rallied to my support. Those who came up here to aid me did me a service I can never forget. . . . I want to thank the Oregon papers for the fairness they showed in telling the whole story. I am glad the Oregon people know all about it, and I feel they sympathize with me."[57]

The verdict was popular with many. Mitchell's attorneys, Morris and Shipley, received a sheaf of telegrams from Oregonians thanking them for their fine work. O. V. Hurt, Mitchell's most important advocate, also praised Mitchell's attorneys. And he singled out Mitchell's other chief defenders: the press, "whose influence was exerted from the first on the side of right and justice," he said, "have aided materially in helping to stamp out this guilty cult from the Northwest. God bless the newspapers of the country."[58]

In Oregon, newspapers rejoiced. The Corvallis *Times* wrote, "In every case there were expressions of approval to the effect that the slayer of the Roller reptile had been set free." The paper took satisfaction that the jury needed little time to reach its verdict, and that the trial had finally made clear the sorry truth about Edmund Creffield. "The result is that the public now knows that it was not religion but complete depravity that was the controlling motive in the life of the roller viper, and that when young Mitchell stung him to death in the streets of Seattle, he ridded the world of one of the biggest devils in it. The wonder is that, doing such things, Creffield was suffered to live so long."[59]

In surprising contrast, the Seattle press was relatively subdued in covering Mitchell's acquittal and his triumphant walk through the downtown city streets. In yet another twist in this odd story, the *Star* and the *Seattle Times* finally showed signs of confronting their own role in this case, and in the process, their enthusiasm for the hero they had created began to wane.

6 Second Thoughts

The time has come when it is going to be necessary to make an example of a few insane persons!

—*SEATTLE TIMES* EDITORIAL, JULY 9, 1906

Don't let's talk so much—or if we must talk, why not do a little thinking at the same time.

—SEATTLE *STAR* EDITORIAL, JULY 17, 1906

O N JULY 7, 1906, near the end of George Mitchell's trial, another murder shook the city of Seattle. For many, this new shooting proved that excusing murder for any reason was a dangerous game that would only encourage even more murders. For the *Seattle Times,* so ardent an apologist for Mitchell's killing of Edmund Creffield, it was a time of reckoning—and for second thoughts about the law and about the responsibility of the press. When yet another murder occurred, on July 12, even the Seattle *Star* was stunned into more circumspect reporting.

These murders jolted the *Times* and the *Star* out of their self-serving sensationalism and forced them to take a more measured approach to the news. Charges that their excessive support for Mitchell had encouraged further lawlessness led to no outright admissions of guilt or regret from either paper, but both substantially changed their general attitude to the courts and to criminal suspects. In a broader sense, the papers' editors seemed to become more aware of the tremendous influence they held over public opinion. It was an important lesson for both newspapers.

Despite their revised attitude toward the law, the *Seattle Times* and the *Star* remained wedded to the traditional notions of family values that had underlain their coverage of the Mitchell-Creffield case. For them, the overriding principles were those of family loyalty, and most of all the responsibility of men to protect their women. The facts of Mitchell's murder of Creffield were only understood within that broader worldview. As new facts emerged, they were again placed and evaluated within this worldview. As such, the press continued serving not only to inform the public, but also to reinforce the conventional gender norms of the day.

The Death of George Meade Emory

The murder on July 7 had no direct connection to the Mitchell-Creffield case. Still, there were enough similarities that it was easy to make a connection between the two cases, and to argue that a cavalier public attitude toward murder in the earlier case had paved the way for another killing. What most gave pause, though, was that the murder victim on July 7 was a prominent Seattle attorney who—unlike Edmund Creffield—would be sorely missed. Murder was far easier to excuse when the victim was a social deviant, such as Creffield, than when he was a member of the city's elite.

In the summer of 1906, Chester Thompson, the nineteen-year-old scion of a prominent Seattle family, had become distraught because his beau, Charlotte Whittlesey, no longer wanted him to call on her. Increasingly obsessed with Whittlesey, Thompson began to stalk her. On the evening of July 7, he thought he saw her enter the home of her uncle, George Meade Emory. A highly successful local attorney, Emory lived with his wife and two young children in a spacious home on Denny Way.

Thompson decided to confront Whittlesey then and there, so he charged into the Emory home. The first person he encountered in the downstairs hallway was Emory himself, whom Thompson suspected had advised Whittlesey to reject him. When Emory attempted to force Thompson to leave the house, the young man shot the attorney twice, then ran upstairs, where he barricaded himself in the nursery with the two young Emory children. Mortally wounded, Emory lingered for several hours before dying. Thompson's father, another prominent local attorney, finally convinced his son to free the children and surrender to police. The *Star* reported that Thompson was believed "to be mentally irresponsible" at the time of the shooting, and his father claimed that his son's mental state had suffered from too much studying and eventually from an obsession over Whittlesey.[1] It was widely expected that Thompson would plead not guilty to the murder, using temporary insanity as his defense.

This case's similarities with the Mitchell-Creffield case quickly became the subject of much talk. Both murderers were young men who believed their victim had wronged them in a way that that justified murder. Thompson's calm demeanor immediately after the shooting—and even after Emory's death—recalled Mitchell's attitude and self-justification after he shot Creffield. Thompson contended, "I only did what was right. I wanted to see the girl and Emory tried to beat me. I shot him in self defense." He added, "It was Emory's fault. He had no right interfering with me. The girl would have married me had it not been for Emory."[2]

For the *Times*, the killing of George Meade Emory was a nightmare. On Monday, July 9, 1906, it published bold headlines on the front page:

SIXTEEN PAGES.   SEATTLE, WASHINGTON, MONDAY EVENING, JULY 9, 1906.   FIVE CENTS EVERYWHERE.

JUDGE EMORY IS DEAD!

WHOLE CITY CRIES OUT FOR **VENGEANCE!**

Murderer Must Not Escape on Plea of Insanity!

COLD BLOODED CRIME MUST BE PUNISHED!

Faced with a clearly unjustifiable murder so similar to the one the paper had lavishly defended before, the *Seattle Times* recanted its earlier canonization of Mitchell. It now contended that the shooting of Creffield had been only "partially justifiable," and, furthermore, it cast doubt on insanity as a defense in a premeditated shooting. In a long editorial on July 9, the paper attacked the insanity defense, warning that "murder will run riot in our city" if agitated young men continued to take the law into their own hands.

Dramatizing its points through the use of boldface type throughout the editorial, the *Times* argued that Chester Thompson had hardly been insane, but rather had very carefully prepared to commit murder:

> Of course **the plea of insanity** will be set up in Thompson's behalf. That's the popular and modern way of defending **murderers**! But Thompson was **sane enough** to get a gun—and **load it**! Thompson was **sane enough** to choose a time of night when he **expected** to find the young woman with her chosen company! Thompson was **sane enough** to leave his hat and coat outside the immediate grounds of Judge Emory's home before entering. He wanted no incumbrances. **Every act** which Thompson performed touching this **murder** was as **sane** as the conduct of any man can be when he starts out to **commit murder**!

The *Times* argued that "the time has come when it is going to be necessary to **make an example of a few insane persons**!" The conclusion of the editorial went beyond the Thompson case to the broader issues raised by that case and the Mitchell-Creffield case:

> It seems to us that the **time has come** when there must be moulded a public opinion that will teach **murderers** and **assassins** that the Mosaic law **will be fulfilled** even in the **Twentieth Century**! It seems to us that the **time has come** when it should be emphatically understood that the man who has passed in the community **as a sane man** cannot **deliberately kill another man** without paying the penalty of the law! . . . If the citizens of Seattle and King County expect to **live in comparative safety** a public opinion must be aroused in this community which will **stay the hand** of

the man **who expects to kill his enemy** and then **escape** under the plea of **insanity!**[3]

The next day, the *Times* observed that "insane murderers are getting to be mighty thick in Seattle," and urged "about a hundred business men had better go insane for half an hour and wreak vengeance on these insane murderers. That would restore sanity in Seattle in twenty-four hours."[4]

The *Times* also noted that the Emory killing might have a "moral influence" on the jury in the Mitchell trial, describing Judge Frater's actions to keep the sequestered jury from being swept up in the emotion following Emory's death. It also reported that the defense had reduced its witness list in order to speed the completion of the trial so that court officers would be free to attend the Emory funeral.[5]

The *Times* did not go so far as to print any explicit self-criticism after Emory's death, and readers would not have gleaned from its denunciations of Thompson any overt contrition over its earlier glorification of Mitchell's murder of Creffield. But the paper had quite clearly changed its view. Even though it did not attack Mitchell directly, it attacked the insanity defense that had been so central to his case. The *Times*'s call for an end to self-appointed "murderers and assassins" applied as much to Mitchell as it did to Thompson.

The paper's second thoughts about George Mitchell were manifested again at the time of Mitchell's acquittal, just three days after Emory's murder. The *Times*'s reaction was far different from what one would have expected given the paper's previous lavish defense of Mitchell. A short editorial cast doubt on Mitchell's insanity, asking, "Now if Mitchell were really insane when he killed Creffield, is he not insane today? And if he be insane today where are the officers who should cause his arrest and incarceration at Steilacoom?" The paper also expressed worry about the potential for even more killings.[6]

Still more telling was the paper's thinly disguised editorial article on its front page praising the prosecution in the Mitchell case. In May, shortly after Mitchell killed Creffield, the *Times* had run a front-page editorial that excoriated the "legal bookworms" who insisted that Mitchell should face trial for murder in the first degree. That editorial had argued that "if there were more men like George Mitchell, there would be fewer human beasts."[7] In July, however, after months of lion-izing Mitchell and minimizing the importance of a strict enforcement of the law, the *Times* now praised Mitchell's chief prosecutor for unre-lenting opposition to self-appointed and self-justified murderers. The piece was given as much prominence as the story recounting Mitch-ell's acquittal, and it characterized Prosecutor Mackintosh as the ideal public servant:[8]

MUCH CREDIT DUE PROSECUTING ATTORNEY

ATTITUDE OF KENNETH MACKINTOSH
IN MITCHELL CASE WAS THAT OF AN ABLE
AND CONSCIENTIOUS OFFICER OF THE LAW

Case of the State Presented Succinctly and Vigorously, as Was the Sworn Duty Entailed Upon Office

Lawyer for the People Brilliantly Assisted by John F. Miller and Every Line of Clever Defense Fought

The article referred to Prosecutor Mackintosh as "a living exem-plar of the stern dignity of the law which forbids the slaying of one man by another save in defense of his very life." It characterized him as a stalwart public official who did his best to "protest against any man taking the law into his own hands, no matter what the provoca-tion, and to demand in the name of law and order, which the society of modern times has set up, that a man who does such a thing should be punished according to the letter of that law which he is sworn to enforce." Mackintosh, said the *Times*, "has been fighting for the law of the land. . . . His examinations, cross-examinations and address to the jury have been splendid examples of the duties of a prosecuting attorney." The paper noted that Macintosh persisted despite a tidal wave of public support for Mitchell (which, the *Times* failed to note, it had helped to precipitate):

He ignored sentiment. He spurned the weakness of pity. He prosecuted the case relentlessly, vigorously, resourcefully and diligently and performed his duty to the whole public regardless of the ideas of any man or community of men."

The *Times* went on to praise Mackintosh for his willingness to go against public sentiment in the case, even if it meant courting "the political oblivion of the dog-catcher's wagon." It also praised his chief deputy, John Miller, for his staunch devotion to the law. The *Times*'s only mention of Mitchell's attorneys was buried in a congratulation to Miller for combating the "cleverly presented" arguments of Morris and Shipley.[9]

The *Times* was not alone in its concern that Mitchell's acquittal might portend further violence. Judge Frater made headlines in the region about a week later, when he publicly condemned the Mitchell verdict as a "disgrace."

> When a jury of twelve men returned a verdict of not guilty in a case where it was clearly proved that the defendant was guilty of a cold blooded murder under the laws, the spectators applauded their act. They made a hero of a man guilty of murder in the eyes of the law and demonstrated their approval when a jury failed to do their duty and freed a murderer.

Frater praised the local prosecutor for attempting to enforce the laws and excoriated the Multnomah County, Oregon, prosecutor for his support of Mitchell. "When an officer of the law in a neighboring State takes such an action it shows that a deplorable spirit of lawlessness is abroad."[10] Frater did not specifically castigate the *Times* or the *Star*, but his indictment of those who "made a hero of a man guilty of murder in the eyes of the law" clearly encompassed their sensational coverage of the case.

The Seattle *Argus*, a weekly paper of commentary and opinion with close ties to the local prosecutor, had never defended Mitchell, so its reaction to the Thompson-Emory case was no surprise. The *Argus* contended that "there is getting to be altogether too much shooting in this world, and having shot, too much sentimentality over the murderers. . . . Let us hang a few of these . . . Harry Thaws, George

Mitchells and Chester Thompsons and revolvers will become a drug on the market." The *Argus* scoffed at the notion that these defendants were really insane, noting that men such as Mitchell, Thaw, and others never were so agitated that they picked the "wrong" man to shoot or missed their mark.

Most of all, the *Argus* worried that the insanity defense had simply made murder an easy and attractive option for angry people. In Mitchell's case, murder followed a sense of outrage at the alleged dishonoring of the perpetrator's sisters. In Thompson's case, the hurdle was even lower—a broken heart, a courtship gone wrong. What would come next? When the "temporary insanity dodge is worked," the *Argus* said, it makes all of human life insecure "because there are others with a private grudge against somebody who may take it out the same way, figuring that they can get off." The price was simply too high to pay, the editor maintained. "All the broken hearts the world ever saw are not worth the life of a man like G. Meade Emory, nor will all the regrets that will ever be expressed bring the breath of life back to his body or cause the closed eye lids to open."[11]

Unlike the *Times*, the Seattle *Star* neither praised the prosecutor nor attacked the insanity defense. Rather, the *Star* offered a front-page article by Chester Thompson's father, describing his son's "mental distress," and noting the "dementia" that grew as Charlotte Whittlesey became increasingly distant from Chester. Still, the *Star*'s coverage of the Mitchell case became much more subdued following Emory's death; its article on Mitchell's acquittal was straightforward and spare, lacking the fulsome verbiage that had characterized the paper's earlier treatment of Mitchell. The *Star* noted that Mitchell's supporters rejoiced at the verdict, but the paper itself offered no comment, and the only picture it ran was of Mitchell's attorney, Will H. Morris.[12]

Within days, however, the *Star* would very explicitly change course in its coverage of the Mitchell case—arguing that he probably should have been convicted at least of a reduced charge. The *Star*'s change of heart came when yet another murder occurred, on Thursday, July 12, 1906.

Esther's Revenge

I did a good deed and want the world to know of it.

—ESTHER MITCHELL

My God, what could the girl have been thinking to do such a terrible thing?

—O. V. HURT

The July 12 killing rocked the city—and even the *Star*—because it seemed so incomprehensible. Just a few days after his triumphant acquittal, George Mitchell was gunned down in a Seattle train station. What was all the more startling was the identity of the murderer: Esther Mitchell. Feigning a willingness to try to reconcile with her brother, she had agreed to see George off as he was about to catch a train to Portland. Following him as he headed for his train, she pulled out a pistol and shot him. As she later recalled, "Then I was walking to the door and George was in front of me. It was just the chance I wanted and I shot him."[13]

Although Mitchell's death caught virtually everyone by surprise, it had been carefully planned by Esther Mitchell and Maud Creffield. Infuriated by George's acquittal and by the outpouring of support for him from the press and the public, they vowed to avenge Creffield's death. As Maud later recounted, "When I heard the jury say not guilty, I went to Esther's room and told her I would kill him."[14] Maud bought a gun at a downtown Seattle store the next day, but she failed to track down George that afternoon.

Both Maud and Esther soon realized that Esther would have a better opportunity to shoot George, particularly because George, her other brothers, and their father all held out hope for a family reconciliation. As Maud later recounted, "Esther said she would do it for me and I told her I would be glad if she would, and that I was determined that he had to die." Esther took Maud's gun, wrapping it in a cloth and hiding it in the bosom of her dress. She then walked to the Union

GEORGE MITCHELL
Murdered yesterday afternoon by his own sister

The murder of George Mitchell by his sister, just days after his acquittal for killing Creffield, stunned the city and reporters. (Seattle Times, 13 July 1906)

Train Station with her brother Fred, to bid farewell to her father and, she hoped, to kill George. George was there, willing to talk to her, but at virtually the last moment, her plan failed. She had wrapped the gun too carefully, and could not unwrap it without giving away her plan.[15] Frustrated and angry, she refused to talk to George, and hurried back to her rooming house, where she hid the gun under her mattress until the next day.

That Thursday afternoon, Esther got a second chance. George and his brother, Perry, were leaving Seattle for Portland, and she returned to the train station. This time she removed the gun from her dress much earlier and hid it under her a coat she was carrying. It was a hot day, but no one seemed suspicious that she had brought a coat along. She walked into the large marble-columned waiting room of the train station shortly after 4 P.M., ostensibly to end her bitter estrangement from her brother and to bid him farewell. They spoke briefly, then she shook hands with him and said, "Good bye." He was disappointed by her coolness and lack of appreciation for all he had done for her, but the train was soon departing, so he turned to leave. It was then that she shot him. George crumpled to the floor. Their brother Fred grabbed Esther, but she did not resist. The report of the gun startled bystanders, and a crowd of several hundred quickly gathered.[16]

The shooting stunned the city. John Miller, the deputy prosecutor, lamented, "My God, have all the people gone crazy?" City police quickly assumed that Maud Creffield was an accomplice or perhaps the mastermind of the crime, and police began to hunt for her. She had gone to Creffield's grave that afternoon, but upon hearing that Mitchell had been shot and that she was wanted, she telephoned police from a drugstore on Broadway. She waited there until a detective arrived and took her to the police station.

City police called in reinforcements to the police station, worrying that the crowd gathering there might turn into a mob; it didn't, but the police were conspicuous in their presence. Police Chief Charles Wappenstein took Esther to his office to question her, but that task required no great effort. She rather proudly proclaimed her great satisfaction in killing her brother:

> I do not regret doing it. I am glad I did it. I fired once and I tried to fire another, but there was such a loud noise made by the crowd I don't know whether I fired again or not. I shot him in the head and I knew if I hit where I intended to it was sure death. I intended to follow him to Portland if I did not shoot him here.[17]

For her part, Maud Creffield was still angry at the press for its support of George Mitchell, so she refused to talk to reporters. "I have never told the reporters anything. They all take George's part and tell such awful things about me that are not true. . . . No, let them go mourn with the dead man whom they praised so much."[18]

The shooting of George Mitchell by his own sister was big news, and the Seattle newspapers once again provided extensive and sensational coverage. The *Times* issued a series of extra editions immediately after Mitchell's death. The first extra hit the street less than thirty minutes after the shooting; it was followed by seven others from the *Times*, as details were added. The fourth extra edition carried heavy, dark headlines, some of them three inches high:

AVENGE
DEATH OF CREFFIELD

The extra edition told the bare facts of the murder, said that police were hunting for Maud Creffield ("if she can be found"), and included a statement from Esther Mitchell that she had determined to kill her brother immediately after his acquittal. As was true for many newspapers of that era, getting the news before competitors seemed to be as important as the news itself. The next day, the *Seattle Times* published an article trumpeting its "scoop" over its rivals.[19]

On July 13—the day after the murder—the *Times* published twelve articles about the tragedy. It also printed photographs of Esther, Maud, and George, and of the waiting room at Union Train Station where George had died. Not to be outdone, that same day the *Star* published seventeen articles and three photographs about the murder.

The great tragedy of sister killing brother made this story particularly compelling. In telling that part of the story, both the *Times* and the *Star* persisted in the mindset that had guided their entire coverage of the case from their very first interview with George Mitchell: the role of men was to protect women, and women should be grateful for that protection. That abiding worldview had guided the *Times* and the *Star* in their reckless defense of George Mitchell, and even as they recanted their facile disregard for the law, both papers continued to defend a broader notion of gender roles.

For both the *Star* and the *Times*, the defining part of the overall story was Mitchell's heroic defense of his sister and her callous disregard for his concern. The *Star* mourned the death of "the brother who risked his life" to save his sister "from the power of a degenerate"—

the "brother who had taken a gambler's chance on legal death to avenge the honor of his sisters." "George Mitchell did the world a service when he ridded it of the Holy Roller leader. His method may be questioned, but the result cannot." The *Times* published an interview with Mitchell's attorneys, Silas Shipley and Will Morris, in which they stressed Mitchell's upright demeanor, describing him as a virtuous young man who never swore or used vulgar expressions. His motives were pure: "His paramount desire was the protection of Esther Mitchell, to whom he had a great attachment, and his older sister, Mrs. Starr, the mother of the three beautiful little children who were so often seen around the court during the trial."[20] The attorneys noted their shock at Esther's revenge:

> Still, it was beyond our comprehension and beyond the comprehension of the public officials to reasonably believe that such a horrible act could be perpetrated by a sister upon a brother who had been willing to sacrifice his life to protect her honor.[21]

Both papers were appalled at Esther's ungratefulness for George's defense of her honor and by her lack of remorse over killing her brother. The *Times* lamented the "unnatural" viciousness of a sister toward a brother, suggesting that Maud had manipulated Esther. On Friday, July 13, the *Times* ran a banner headline on its front page:

In half-inch-high print, near the top of the page, the paper printed Esther's defiant admission of guilt:

"THE REASON I KILLED GEORGE WAS THAT HE HAD KILLED AN INNOCENT MAN, AND RUINED MY REPUTATION BY STATING THAT CREFFIELD HAD SEDUCED ME."[22]

The *Star* stressed the horror of Esther's ingratitude and malice: "That he was of her flesh and blood adds fuel to the indignation and that she killed him for his efforts to save her shows a lack of so many human sentiments as to indicate madness."[23] The *Times* followed a similar theme, pointing out the great tragedy of a young girl betraying the brother who had saved her from Creffield's clutches:

> Shorn of every sentiment of sisterly affection by the teachings of a false prophet, Esther Mitchell yesterday killed the brother who had jeopardized his life to save her honor. Proudly posing as an angel of vengeance, this young girl hypocritically murdered George Mitchell, a few hours after the story of the outrages which Franz Edmund Creffield practiced upon his women victims had impelled a jury to declare the brother not guilty of the murder of the religious fanatic.[24]

The *Star*'s most moving story told of a sister's betrayal:

HER GOOD-BYE WAS
A MISSILE OF DEATH

From the shadow of the gallows, George Mitchell walked to his death yesterday afternoon. Mitchell was shot and instantly killed at 4:20 o'clock by his sister, Esther, for whose honor he had taken human life. . . . Treacherous, she came to say "goodbye" and with a smile on her lips and a spirit that shammed forgiveness, walked up behind the brother who had risked so much for her sake and coolly sent a bullet crashing through his head. Her errand of mis-styled vengeance finished, the girl sank into a seat of the waiting room and threw the still smoking gun to the floor.

With murder in her heart, and all the details arranged with Satanic cleverness, Miss Mitchell went to the station, at the last moment as it were, pretending that she had come to extend sisterly well-wishes and a last God-speed to the brother whom she might never see again. Not a hitch occurred to mar the success of her plan. With the body of her victim shrouded on the marble slab at the morgue, she expressed satisfaction with it all. No remorse, no regret, no emotion followed the consummation of the plot. It was as if everything human had been blotted from her being, and she had become a cold, heartless, calculating murderess.[25]

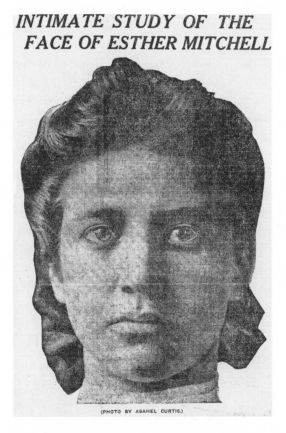

INTIMATE STUDY OF THE FACE OF ESTHER MITCHELL

(PHOTO BY ASAHEL CURTIS.)

The press was repelled and fascinated by Esther's shooting of her brother. Reporters labeled her actions "unnatural" and wondered how she could remain so calm follow George's death. (Seattle Star, 13 July 1906)

For the *Times* and the *Star*, Esther's villainy was all the worse because her demeanor remained so cool. The *Star* noted in a headline that on her first night in jail, Esther "Sleeps the Sleep of a Care-Free Girl." It reported that jailers kept a vigil at Esther's cell, fearing that she might try to commit suicide. She surprised them; rather than appearing agitated, she seemed at peace. "Not once during the night did she murmur. For her there were no horror dreams." A *Times* reporter described his interview with Esther at the jail, noting that she confessed to the murder "as calmly as though discussing some event of most ordinary character. . . . Question upon question had been asked and answered, and the seriousness of her position had been emphasized as well as the unnaturalness of what she had done. Yet never did a person appear more at ease than did she." The reporter also noted that jail officials were amazed by the calm attitudes displayed by both Esther and Maud. "Crime is an old story to these officers of the law but never in all their experience had they to do with prisoners who are as indifferent to what the future may have in store for them as are Esther Mitchell and Maud Creffield."[26]

Even while the *Times* and the *Star* were praising George Mitchell and excoriating Esther and Maud, they were stunned by what the *Times* referred to as a "murder mania" in the city. The murder of the distinguished jurist George Meade Emory in the closing day of Mitchell's trial had given pause to both papers. Perhaps recognizing that their celebration of Mitchell had contributed to a growing lawlessness in the city, both newspapers earnestly differentiated between the killings of Creffield and of Mitchell. The *Star*, for example, maintained that the "reptile" Creffield deserved death, while Mitchell did not. In contrast with Mitchell's removal of a menace to society, said the *Star*, there was no justifiable reason for Esther to kill her brother. "The motive of Esther Mitchell and the character of her victim bring universal condemnation."[27]

Despite its continued defense of George Mitchell, the *Star* clearly had second thoughts about some aspects of his case. Without any acknowledgement of its new tack or of the irony involved, the *Star* carried an editorial advising, "Let's Think When We Talk." It observed that most had applauded Mitchell's shooting of Creffield, had hoped for acquittal, and had been pleased at the verdict. His murder,

THE SEATTLE STAR

BY STAR PUBLISHING CO. 1307 and 1309 Seventh Ave.

EVERY AFTERNOON EXCEPT SUNDAY.

Telephones—
Editorial: Independent 575; Sunset Main 1050.
Business: Independent 1138; Sunset, Main 1050.

BALLARD STAR AGENCY—321 Ballard Ave. Sunset, Rallard 306.

One cent per copy, six cents per week, or twenty-five cents per month. Delivered by mail or carrier. No free copies.

TO MAIL SUBSCRIBERS—The date when your subscription expires is on the address label of each paper. When that date arrives, if your subscription has not again been paid in advance, your name is taken from the list. A change of date on the address label is a receipt.
Entered at the Postoffice at Seattle, Washington, as second-class matter.

Let's Think When We Talk

One of our greatest faults as a people is that we talk too much.

When George Mitchell killed Creffield we went about telling each other what a good thing it was.

Most of us expressed the wish that Mitchell would not be punished.

And when he was acquitted most of us expressed gratification thereat. Since Mitchell was acquitted there have been more killings and now we are going about regretting his acquittal and expressing in a most emphatic way our belief that these killings wouldn't have followed if Mitchell had only been sent to the penitentiary.

But worst of all we are loud in our declaration that some one must hang. It doesn't much matter who it is, but we must have a hanging.

There are altogether too many shootings, we declare, and the only way to put a stop to these incidents is to string somebody up.

If we'd all quit talking for a while and allow the juries to determine what should be done with these people who are accused of murder we would be much better off.

If there is anyone deserving of death by hanging or of imprisonment for life or for a long term of years wouldn't it be a good idea to allow the courts to so determine.

Let the young man and the two women now in the King County jail, charged with murder, be tried for the crimes which they committed and not for all the murders that have been committed in King county during the last year.

And let's be done with this crying out for someone to hang. Let's be fair and if the courts say that anyone now up in the King County jail must be punished by death or by long imprisonment let us allow the sentence to be imposed without criticism or applause.

Don't let's talk so much—or if we must talk, why not do a little thinking at the same time?

however, had convinced many that perhaps he should have served at least a short term in prison, as that might have saved his life. Others, angry about his murder, were starting to argue for revenge. Worried about these swings in public opinion, the *Star* told its readers to leave the law to the courts. "Don't let us talk so much—or if we must talk, why not do a little thinking at the same time." The *Times* observed that local "officers of the law are appalled at the series of capital crimes which has found its last chapter in the murder of George Mitchell by his sister." The *Times* itself commented that "Seattle seems to be in the grip of a mania of murder. Homicide is epidemic."[28]

In sharp contrast to their earlier coverage before Mitchell's trial, the *Times* and the *Star* gave extensive coverage to local officials who condemned those who took the law into their own hands. The difference was particularly notable in the *Star,* which had previously ridiculed the local prosecutor for insisting on going after Mitchell. The *Times* gave prominent play to assistant prosecuting attorney John Miller's attack on vigilante activity:

> As long as public sentiment is in this maudlin condition, no man's life is safe and law and order is a farce. When a man can deliberately shoot another in the back and be acquitted, simply because a woman is mixed up in the case, it is time to stop this rot about honor. What is going to become of us? What are the courts for? This is no mining camp. We claim it is a civilized community. Yet, what can we do, with public sentiment of this sort. The police can arrest murderers and we can prosecute them, but we can't get a jury to punish them. This is all wrong, and it is a very serious matter.[29]

The *Times* also published an interview with the county's deputy coroner, who argued that juries were too lenient.

> This thing of allowing men and women to kill in Seattle should be stopped some way. I don't believe in hanging a crazy man, no matter what he does, but I don't believe he should be allowed to commit murder and then be turned loose because the jury finds

that he was crazy. Such verdicts under the present condition of the law are bound to encourage crime.[30]

The *Times* also quoted Seattle Police Chief Wappenstein's statement that juries should have more respect for the law: "This thing is going too far. It is the fault of the juries. We do our duty: the prosecuting attorney works hard and does his full duty—and the jury lets them go. What's the use?" Wappenstein captured well the contradictory feelings of many, however, when he admitted that he would have voted to acquit Mitchell if he had been in the jury. "I think Creffield ought to have been killed." Like many others in legal circles, he was frustrated by having to deal with any of this at all. "At any rate," he said, "I wish these Oregon people would kill each other on their own side of the river."[31]

Adding further to the turmoil over the insanity defense were the results of George Mitchell's autopsy, which disclosed that his brain was quite normal. Any chronic insanity would have been evident in the shape of the brain, the medical examiners noted. The *Star* proclaimed that the autopsy thus showed that "he was as sane as any ordinary person when he shot Edmund Creffield."[32]

Consistent with its earlier coverage of Creffield's death, Seattle's other major daily newspaper, the *Seattle Post-Intelligencer*, was far more subdued than the *Times* or the *Star* in reporting on Mitchell's death. The *Post-Intelligencer* carried no bold headlines describing "wanton" acts or a "missile of death." Instead, the paper's relatively small headline on the murder carried the barest of facts:[33]

GEORGE MITCHELL KILLED BY SISTER

The corresponding article focused chiefly on the facts of the case. There were no articles or editorials addressing the broader issues of law and order, no condemnation of "murder mania." Unlike the *Times* and the *Star*, the *Post-Intelligencer* had no need for such public hand-wringing, for its editors had not helped to inflame public opinion in the first place.

Yet even with its more subdued approach, the *Post-Intelligencer* could not avoid being caught up in the wave of emotion engendered by the latest act in what the paper called "the second chapter of a tragedy which has not yet seen its end."[34] It gave more extensive coverage to Mitchell's death than it had to Creffield's, and printed, along with a picture of a crowd gathered at the police station to catch a glimpse of Esther, photos of George Mitchell, Esther Mitchell, Perry Mitchell, and Maud Creffield. The photos themselves are haunting, even a century later, for their solemn-faced calm belies the anger and turmoil that marked the lives of those young people.

Like the afternoon newspapers, the *Post-Intelligencer* was shocked by the death of a young man at the hand of his sister. Commenting that "the evil that men do lives after them," it reported that Creffield's influence had poisoned Esther's "natural instinct."[35] It noted, too, that Creffield's baneful influence also still affected Esther's sister, Donna Starr, who seemed happy at the news of the slaying.

In Oregon, the press praised George Mitchell's sacrifice while sadly recounting Esther's great betrayal. In Corvallis, the *Gazette* wrote that the report of Mitchell's murder "sent a shiver of horror over all who listened to the direful news." The murder also bode ill for the town so long afflicted by Creffield. "Whether Creffield's influence or Holy Rollerism will end even now, is a matter seriously doubted by a majority of Corvallis people familiar with the history of the cult," the paper noted. A newspaper correspondent wrote that George Mitchell was seen as a hero in Corvallis, "and his murder at the hands of his sister is universally condemned." O. V. Hurt, Maud Creffield's long-suffering father, nearly collapsed when notified of the murder, and when he recovered, he lamented Esther's deed: "My God, what could the girl have been thinking to do such a terrible thing?" The Corvallis *Times* observed that "The slaying of George Mitchell by his sister, melancholy tragedy that it is, is a small part of the legacy left to this country by the late Mr. Creffield. When the roll of the damned is made up, if the distinguished name of Creffield is not found far up toward the head of the list and the illustrious Edmund himself a chief bower at the right hand of the devil, then hell is not what it is cracked up to be and the scheme of eternal punishments a misfit."[36]

In Portland, the Multnomah County prosecuting attorney, John

Manning, praised George Mitchell as "a nice, steady young fellow," and said, "I am very sorry to learn of his death." Showing little awareness of how he himself, by his very public support for Mitchell, might have contributed to this cycle of killing, Manning again praised the young man for murdering Creffield, saying that he had acted "as any other decent man anywhere" would have done. Manning assailed Esther as "utterly depraved" for shooting her brother, "especially in view of what her brother did for her. . . . I regret very much that young Mitchell died, and I want to see his sister justly punished for her crime."[37]

While most newspaper editors and local officials bemoaned the breakdown of law and order, the common people of Seattle were moved to pay their respects to the young man from Oregon whose self-appointed errand of honor had brought him death. Hundreds came to view his body at the Bonney-Watson funeral home in Seattle. The Seattle *Star* observed that women, men, and children of all classes and ages quietly filed past Mitchell's body, which was surrounded by dozens of bouquets of flowers of sweet peas, nasturtiums, and other flowers commonly found in home gardens. The crowd, the *Star* reported, was motivated by a sense of loss and sadness rather than by morbid curiosity. "Nearly everyone displayed a grief at the human tragedy unveiled in such a terrible climax. The women were especially affected, many breaking into tears." Among those who came to view the body was the mysterious "flower woman" from his trial. On Thursday evening, shortly after the news of George's shooting sped through the city, she had stopped by the police station to see if the news was correct—and then, to ask where the body was. She had gone alone to the morgue on Thursday evening and stared silently at the body. On Friday she returned, again alone, dressed in white from head to toe, with a huge bouquet that she place on George's chest.[38]

George's brothers, Perry and Fred, were heartbroken, nearly penniless, and uncertain if they would be able to afford to take George's body back to Oregon for burial. The *Star* reported that many of its readers asked to contribute to a burial fund, so the paper began to take donations. By Monday morning, the paper had collected $130.20. The funeral home discounted its $126 bill, saying it would accept $50 for all its expenses. The *Star* then gave the remaining money to Fred and Perry, to cover travel expenses, a funeral in Newberg, and, the paper hoped, a headstone for George Mitchell. Fred and Perry caught the 11:15 A.M. train to Newberg on Monday, and as they left, they told the *Star* to thank the people of Seattle for their generosity. "We were almost without funds when George was killed, and without assistance we would have been unable to bury our brother beside the grave of our mother." George's simple casket, covered with flowers from Seattle residents, was placed in the baggage car.[39]

George's burial took place the next day, Tuesday, July 17. A large crowd gathered at the Newberg train station that morning to meet the flower-bedecked coffin and the grief-stricken brothers. After a Friends service conducted by Mrs. M. E. K. Edwards, an old Mitchell family friend, at the W.W. Hollingsworth undertaking parlor, George's body was taken to the Friends Cemetery in town, and—"with a few last words"—was buried. "Beside his mother in a quiet cemetery of the Friends church, George Mitchell lies in the last long rest," reported the Corvallis *Times*. The townspeople of Newberg had also taken up a collection to help pay for the funeral and to provide enough money for Perry and Fred to return to Portland after the service. The mayor and the town marshal, both of whom had gone to Seattle for George's trial, personally solicited the funds.[40]

In writing about the funeral, one Oregon newspaper attempted to explain how a brother and sister could have come to such a bitter end. The Albany *Weekly Herald* observed that their problems had really begun with the death of their mother. Their eccentric father had essentially abandoned the children, forcing them to fend for themselves. "It is believed that had their mother lived to care for them they would have turned out differently and the horrors lately chronicled would have been averted." The Newberg *Graphic* reported that "the belief is prevalent" among people in the town who knew the family when they had lived in Newberg, that if George's mother had survived to care for her children, "the awful record that has been made by them would have been averted."[41]

Though the *Graphic* made a good point, neither it nor other newspapers had the self-awareness to examine their own role in the long Creffield saga. In Oregon, the press had done much to create an environment in which Creffield's murder seemed not only permissible

but a good idea. In Seattle, sensational newspaper coverage had likewise helped to justify murder, gain an acquittal for George Mitchell,
and further poison his relationship with his sister. By making George
Mitchell a newspaper hero, the Seattle press had helped goad Esther
Mitchell and Maud Creffield into seeking his destruction.

7 Unforgiven

Does this mean that any person may kill another and then go scot free
by pleading insanity?

B Y LATE JULY 1906, the Seattle press had generally lost interest
in the Mitchell-Creffield case. During the ten days immediately
after George Mitchell's death, the *Seattle Times* and the *Star* had
vied with one another in printing stories about Maud Creffield's evil
influence on Esther Mitchell, Mitchell's heartbroken brothers, the generous donations to pay for George's burial in Oregon, and sad accounts
of those final rites. As many as a half-dozen articles per day appeared
in each paper, dominating the front page, some illustrated with photographs or drawings. But then, rather suddenly, what had been a daily
front-page story became a much less frequent one, often consigned to
the inside pages. During a four-month period of 1906, from August 1
through November 30, the *Seattle Times* published just eleven articles
about the Mitchell-Creffield saga, and the *Star* fourteen.

For the most part, the Mitchell-Creffield case had become yesterday's news. Developments in the case were few. Reporters had few
fresh sources for news, as Maud Creffield and Esther Mitchell, still angry
over the papers' adulatory treatment of George Mitchell, granted no
interviews. The continuing story focused primarily on the sanity of the
two women, and lacked the drama of Creffield's murder or of George
Mitchell's trial and murder. Most importantly, as the *Star* observed,
the public was losing interest in the case.[1] With public interest low,

neither the *Star* nor the *Times* devoted great energy to the story. When the story did resurface, however, both papers briefly returned to their bold headlines and passionate coverage.

Other news was capturing the attention of the *Star* and the *Times*, and of the Seattle reading public. In late summer and early autumn of 1906, the *Star* launched a crusade on tax inequities—"How the Poor Man Pays the Rich Man's Taxes"—and began to promote several measures the voters faced in the September 12 city election. The *Times*, too, focused on the ballot measures, taxes, and streetcar franchises, and on promoting a "Made in Seattle Day" to showcase locally produced goods.[2]

In the coverage that the *Times* and the *Star* did provide of the ongoing Mitchell-Creffield story in the autumn of 1906, they were insistent that Esther and Maud should be punished. Both papers had become stalwart in their defense of law and order after the deaths of George Meade Emory and George Mitchell; adding to their ardor was their sense that Esther and Maud had deeply violated the natural order. Murder alone was wrong, but murder of a brother who had defended the honor of a sister was all the worse.

Insanity

Just two days after George Mitchell's funeral, the *Newberg Graphic* editorialized that "All the Holy Roller lunatics should be rounded up and landed in asylums for the insane where they belong."[3] The *Graphic*'s view reflected that of many who believed that only insanity—of Esther and Maud—could account for the tragic murder of George Mitchell. This issue soon emerged in Seattle, too, as local law officials publicly battled over what to do with the two women. In July, during one of Esther Mitchell's first court appearances, Superior Court Judge A. W. Frater—who had presided over George Mitchell's trial—revealed that he wanted to avoid holding a trial for the two women. Worried about prosecution costs and wary that a jury might find them innocent by reason of temporary insanity, Frater invoked a little-used state statute that allowed for the deportation of insane persons who were residents of other states. The judge proposed that

WHICH IS THE CRAZY MAN?

A Seattle Times *editorial cartoon assailed Frater's insanity commission, contending that the real "insanity" stemmed from judges who protected murderers from the police.* (Seattle Times, *21 September 1906*)

a sanity commission be convened and that, if it found the women insane, they be sent back to Oregon.[4]

The prosecutors and the press vehemently opposed Frater's plan. Prosecutor Kenneth Mackintosh and his deputy, John Miller, argued that the two women should face trial for murder and that only a jury could decide on questions of sanity. Miller insisted that a preliminary examination of Esther showed that she "was in her right mind and realized perfectly what she was doing when she murdered her brother." He promised a "strong" prosecution. The outraged Mackintosh contended that Frater's plan sent a terrible message to criminals, indicating that the county would rather save some money than prosecute people who committed murder within its boundaries.[5] In their newfound zeal for rigorous enforcement of the law, the *Seattle Times* and the *Star* readily agreed with the prosecutors, arguing that neither Maud nor Esther should be allowed to escape the full responsibility for their deeds through a subterfuge of insanity. The *Star* insisted that the two women were quite sane:

They knew what they were doing, knew that they were committing a crime for which they might go to the gallows. They have admitted this. They schemed for two days prior to the killing, waiting and watching for an opportunity. Nothing was done on the impulse of the moment. Calmly and deliberately, Esther Mitchell walked up to her brother, hiding beneath her cloak the weapon of death.[6]

Throughout the autumn of 1906, the battle over Maud Creffield and Esther Mitchell was waged in both the courtroom and the press. In September, Judge Frater appointed a commission of three local physicians to ascertain the sanity of the two women. The press gave extensive coverage to the prosecutors' objections to the commission, interviewing Mackintosh and Miller and detailing Miller's arguments in court. Neither paper printed interviews with Judge Frater or with attorneys for Esther or Maud. The coverage focused distinctly on the opponents of Frater's deportation plan.[7]

The commission began its hearings on September 12, 1906, and concluded its work a week later, after examining twenty-six witnesses. The witnesses were divided: some (including Maud's father, O. V. Hurt) believed that the women were insane, while others (such as the police) pointed out their calm demeanor at the time of the shooting and in the weeks afterward.[8] Maud and Esther themselves denied they were insane, explaining that they had acted under divine instruction. In the immediate aftermath of Mitchell's murder, however, they had spoken only in terms of simple revenge, much as George Mitchell had done after killing Creffield. Why their story changed is not clear, although obviously a claim of a divine order would be much more consonant with insanity than simple revenge. Maud Creffield said that God had called her to avenge her husband's death. When further revelation from God directed that Esther "was the chosen one," Maud had obediently stepped aside. She regretted nothing, believing that her role in Mitchell's death had been divinely ordained. Maud also told the physicians that she had contemplated committing suicide on several occasions "and would do so if God so willed." Esther Mitchell maintained that her brother deserved to be punished and that God had clearly outlined her duty to her: "When I was told by God it was my duty to kill him, I was glad. It was not hard to do for I was given strength. At first I felt burdened before I did it, but I soon realized it was God's will and He would care for me. If I had not done it, I would have suffered. I had never shot a pistol before, but was not afraid."[9]

Based on this testimony, the commission unanimously ruled that the two women were insane at the time of Mitchell's murder, and that they continued to suffer from "a form of insanity commonly classified as paranoia, which has its origin in structural defects of the nervous system." The physicians said that the two women remained a danger to themselves and to the public and "should be placed under restraint in an institution for the proper treatment of such cases."[10]

The press trumpeted Mackintosh's outrage at this decision. He told reporters that the commission was illegal and that he would fight the deportation plan. "No court has a right to free them and make life unsafe in this community," he said, promising to enlist the state supreme court to force Judge Frater to put the two women on trial. "No insanity commission can prevent me from trying to bring assassins to justice. If a jury wishes to turn them loose that is their province."[11] The press also highlighted Deputy Prosecutor Miller's attack on the commission:[12]

SAYS EXAMINATION WAS ONLY A FARCE

John F. Miller Charges Mitchell-Creffield Insanity Commission With Deciding Upon Verdict Before the Examination Began--Commission Declares Its Belief That Both Women Were and Are Insane.

The *Seattle Times* joined in the attack. The paper, once a staunch defender of George Mitchell, no longer had any tolerance for casual uses of the insanity defense. The paper worried that the two women might escape prosecution and that the "death of George Mitchell at his sister's hand will go unavenged."[13]

In a front-page editorial, the *Times* made clear its view on the commission's findings:

INSANITY EXCUSE AROUSES MUCH INDIGNATION
LEGAL WAY IS OPENED FOR AN EPIDEMIC OF MURDER

Throughout the city is heard the strongest condemnation of the Mitchell-Creffield insanity proceedings. "A travesty of justice" is one of the mildest expressions used. Everywhere the question is asked: "Does this not mean that any person may kill another and then go scot free by pleading insanity?"[14]

Two days later, another *Times* headline declared:

MURDERERS MUST BE TRIED
MR. MACKINTOSH WILL ASK SUPREME COURT TO COMPEL JUDGE FRATER TO KEEP SLAYERSOF MITCHELL IN KING COUNTY
Endeavors to Avert Miscarriage of Justice

The *Times* also published a front-page editorial cartoon captioned "Which is the Crazy Man?" that showed a judge preventing the sheriff from arresting a murderer—by giving the murderer a "certificate of insanity"; other certificates of insanity abound, floating on the ground and stuffed in the judge's pocket. In the gruesome cartoon; a murder victim lies in the background, and the murderer carries a large knife dripping with blood.[15]

Once the public posturing was done, however, the *Star* and the *Times* paid little attention to the legal battle between Frater and the prosecutor's office over Maud Creffield's and Esther Mitchell's fate. There was little to tell. Both sides sent briefs outlining their views to the state supreme court, but there was no public hearing. Mackintosh and Miller asked the state supreme court for a "writ of prohibition" against Frater's deportation order, arguing that the judge had "acted in excess of his jurisdiction" and delegated too much power to the commission, thus rendering "the entire proceeding void." In response, Frater and the attorneys for Esther and Maud argued that the commission was absolutely necessary to ensure that insane persons were not placed on trial for their lives, and that Frater had given the commission just enough power to fulfill its task. They also argued that Frater, burdened with a heavy workload, had little choice but to delegate the questioning to a qualified panel.[16]

Within a few weeks, the state supreme court asked for further briefs on the constitutionality of the deportation statute itself. The justices were concerned that the statute seemed to assume that a Washington State official escorting a deportee could retain custody of that person even after the pair had left the state. Because state power ended at the border, the statute seemed to be mandating an impossible—and thus unconstitutional—action. The court's request was somewhat unusual, because none of the parties in the case had questioned the statute's constitutionality. As the court later said, the issue "occurred to us while in consultation. Being a question of public importance which might disturb friendly relations with a sister state, the majority of the court believed that it should be carefully considered."[17]

Both sides responded quickly. Judge Frater and the attorneys for the two women argued that the issue of constitutionality was irrelevant because none of the original briefs had raised it. In contrast, Mackintosh and Miller eagerly picked up the argument that the statute was unconstitutional because it was unenforceable. At the "moment" the state official left the state, the court ordering the deportation no longer had power over the deportee, so the deportation act itself could not be executed. In a separate brief, the state's attorney general agreed that the act was unconstitutional because the state lost all legal control when the deportee left the state.[18]

Maud Creffield

Just as these arguments seemed to be moving the Mitchell-Creffield saga to a more conventional legal plane, the case took yet another jarring turn in mid-November. Worn down by the travails of the preceding three and a half years, Maud Hurt Creffield committed suicide. Despite her firm avowal that she was proud of her part in Mitchell's slaying, Maud was deeply depressed. Her spiritual leader and husband was dead, his promised resurrection nowhere in sight, his flock scattered. She was guilt-ridden over the pain that her parents had endured because of her, and she had told the insanity commission that she had frequently contemplated suicide.

On the evening of November 16, 1906, Maud and Esther had been in a common room in the women's ward at the King County jail, playing cards with other inmates. Shortly after 10 P.M., the two women returned to the cell they shared. A few minutes later, another inmate passed the cell and saw the two women embracing one another. About a half hour later, piercing screams from that cell aroused the other inmates, who summoned the jailers. Hurrying to the cell, they found Maud, her face distorted with pain, clutching at her heart. She asked for a drink of water; after drinking, she lost consciousness and soon died.[19]

Suspecting suicide, the sheriff and his deputy made a careful search of the cell, but found no poison. The lack of poison, coupled with the deputy coroner's statement that Maud probably died from heart disease, led the regional newspapers to announce that Maud had died of natural causes. Maud's father, O. V. Hurt, recounted his last visit with her just a few days before her death. He said that he had found her "despondent and depressed" over the delay in the deportation case, but that she would not have committed suicide. "I think she died from grief and a broken heart. When Creffield was killed, Maud felt that all her life had been taken from her and she thought so until her death. She told us repeatedly she had nothing more to live for." Hurt also reported that Maud had told her mother to bury her next to Creffield if she died. Hurt said he believed his daughter would have survived if the courts had moved faster and if she had been sent to an asylum rather than to jail.[20] Esther Mitchell denied that Maud had committed suicide; indeed, she seemed surprised by Maud's sudden death and cried uncontrollably as her friend died in her arms.

Within several days, however, the theories of a natural death were challenged by chemical analysis showing that Maud had taken strychnine. How Maud got the poison was unclear, but suspicion fell on a cousin who had visited her two days before her death. The cousin denied giving poison to Maud, saying that even though Maud wanted to die, she would never commit suicide. "But for the fact that it was cow-

THIRD FATALITY IN HOLY ROLLER DRAMA

Maud Creffield Expires Suddenly in Her Cell at the County Jail--Heart Disease Said to be Cause of Death, Although Autopsy Reveals This Organ in Good Condition.

MAUD CREFFIELD.

*Maud Creffield's death—an apparent suicide—brought the Creffield-Mitchell case back to public attention in November 1906 and undermined Esther Mitchell's mental health. (*Seattle Star, *17 November 1906)*

ardly and that God had forbidden her to commit suicide, Mrs. Creffield often said she would like to kill herself, for she had no desire to live. But she always told me that it was her duty, to live and meet whatever punishment was given to her, and declared she was going to do it."[21]

Jail officials contested the coroner's finding, defensively arguing that they searched every person and package that came to the jail.

"We are very careful about such things," said the chief jailer, "and persons who are liable to kill themselves, as well as everyone else, are closely watched at the time they are here. Mrs. Creffield's cell was searched only a few days ago, and we are certain there was no poison concealed anywhere at that time."[22]

Maud's sudden death propelled her back into the news—both the *Seattle Times* and the *Star* gave front-page coverage to the story. They recounted the details surrounding her death and used the occasion to refer once more to some of the broader beliefs that had long shaped their reporting, wondering:

> What influence congealed the natural fountains of sisterly affection in Esther Mitchell; what stimulant to perversion so prejudiced her mind to kill the brother who had sought only to save her from worse than death, steeled her heart and strengthened her hand , to cold-blooded fratricide?

The paper wrote of the "unspeakable" Creffield, described Maud's and Esther's belief in Creffield's holiness as "blasphemy," and concluded that Maud was controlling the "strange" Esther through hypnotism or some personal magnetism that arose from "the madness of frenzied religion." The *Times* concluded its first story on Maud's death by noting that her death "will save the county several thousands of dollars, as it would have cost considerable to have tried her in case the supreme court overrules the finding of the insanity commission." In similar fashion, the *Star* recounted Maud's "hypnotic power" over Esther. The paper extended no sympathy to Esther, though. Indeed, it held that Esther, despite her denials, had been an accessory to Maud's suicide. The paper concluded that "the girl's horrified expressions of grief as she held the dying woman's head in her lap were merely the utterings of a consummate actress."[23]

Maud's funeral, on November 19 at the Bonney Watson funeral home, was a simple one. Wishing to avoid the crowds that had come to view the bodies of Creffield and Mitchell after their deaths, Maud's family directed that only a few invited guests could view the body or attend the services. O. V. Hurt led the family mourners. Also present were George Mitchell's attorneys, Will Morris and Silas Shipley,

Esther's attorney, W. A. Holzheimer, and Esther herself, accompanied by a deputy sheriff and a police matron. Judge Frater had given Esther permission to attend the funeral, but not the burial at Lakeview Cemetery. The *Seattle Times* described Esther's wrenching goodbye to her friend and close companion:

> It was at the end of the service, when the handful of friends and relatives of the dead woman were asked to take their final leave, that Esther Mitchell stepped in front of the neat but inexpensive casket . . . and bowing over the glass inclosure, looked pitifully for a moment on the dead face and wept loudly. . . . She gazed steadfastly at the casket a moment and then burst into tears, crying loudly but never uttering an audible word. Her eyes were for awhile so steadily fixed on the corpse that they seemed to be glued there. After a time she was led away to a carriage in waiting and returned to the county jail.[24]

At Lakeview Cemetery, Maud was buried next to her infamous husband.

Maud's death left Esther alone to await the supreme court's decision on Judge Frater's plan to send her back to Oregon. In January 1907, the court announced its decision, handing down a mixed verdict: the commission was legitimate, but the deportation law was not. Five of the seven justices agreed on the first point. Writing for the majority, Justice Herman D. Crow observed, "Knowingly placing an insane person on trial for a crime punishable by death is a procedure not to be tolerated by the courts of any civilized nation." Criminal courts, he added, had "an inherent power" to ascertain the sanity of defendants in capital cases. Therefore, Frater's actions in appointing the commission were well within his powers.[25] There was no clear-cut victory for Judge Frater, however, because six of the seven justices ruled that the deportation statute was unconstitutional. Adopting the argument made by Mackintosh and the state's attorney general, the supreme court ruled that the statute simply was not enforceable because Washington State officials lost legal authority as soon as they left the state. Anything done by the sheriff outside the state "would be without authority, as our statutes can have no extra-territorial force."[26]

The seventh justice, Milo A. Root, took no position on the statute because neither party to the case had contested its constitutionality.

In mid-February, Judge Frater signed commitment papers sending Esther Mitchell to the Western Washington Hospital for the Insane. She spent two years there and was released on March 28, 1909; hospital discharge records indicate she her condition as "Recovered." She moved back to Oregon—to the Newport area—where she lived with the family of O. V. Hurt until she married in early 1914. She had not escaped the despair and tragedy that had tracked the principals in the Mitchell-Creffield case, however. On June 12, 1914, at age twenty-six, she took her own life. Like Maud Creffield before her, she used strychnine.[27]

8 News and Values

SHORTLY AFTER GEORGE MITCHELL'S ACQUITTAL, O.V. Hurt had publicly thanked the press—"God bless the newspapers"—for their support of the young murderer. Maud Hurt Creffield, in contrast, had had nothing good to say about the press—much less to reporters, with whom she refused to speak altogether. Although they differed so radically in their sentiments, both father and daughter recognized the great importance the press had played in the Mitchell trial and in the three-year-long Creffield saga.

Hundreds of newspaper articles and editorials, in Corvallis and Seattle alone, had told a story of the volatile mix of religion, sex, violence, and notions of honor. The press in both towns had fostered cynicism about the law and had encouraged resistance to religious experimentation and to social change—such as the push for gender equality—that challenged traditional social norms. The story of Edmund Creffield, George and Esther Mitchell, and all those associated with them is fascinating in its own right, but at least as fascinating is the parallel story of the power of the press to define news in a way that far transcended those events. News, under the guise of a report on the day's happenings, became a broader affirmation of a particular set of values.

In Corvallis, the press told a story that exalted community solidarity and obligations above other considerations. Creffield's first great transgression was that he threatened the town's ambitions for growth and prosperity. The Corvallis press, borrowing from and reinforcing much of what passed for wisdom in contemporary medicine and society, also told its readers that women were inherently weak. The Seattle press, free from civic embarrassment but driven by the lucrative promise of a good story, focused on the human drama of the Creffield saga. This was a story that transcended Creffield and the Mitchells, for it went to the heart of family obligations and even to the very essence of being a man. In the Seattle papers the larger lesson was clear: men had an obligation to protect and defend their female relatives; those women, in turn, owed gratitude to their protectors. These mutual obligations grew out of men's natural strength and women's many weaknesses. This clear invocation of very traditional family values, circa 1900, was grafted onto the news about Creffield, and the Mitchell-Creffield case thus transcended the "facts" of the situation and became a larger lesson about social values.

The press in Seattle and Corvallis also reminded readers about family responsibility and obligation. Because George Mitchell, in killing Creffield, had done his "duty" both as a man and as a brother, he should be able to expect his sisters' gratitude and support. Esther's hostility toward him—first testifying willingly against him, then murdering him—violated the very essence of family obligations and rendered her "a queer psychological problem."[1] The press told its readers that such sibling discord violated the natural order of things and was, quite literally, "beyond comprehension."[2] George, on the other hand, had lived up to his family obligations by killing Creffield; moreover, his unilateral determination of what was best for his sisters made him the personification of manhood. The *Times* reported, "The youth has become a man."[3] The press saw his stoicism as another element of manliness, and commented favorably on Mitchell's unemotional approach to both murder and trial. Only the sad tale of his sister Donna's desertion of husband and children could—in the *Times*'s phrase—"unman" Mitchell, who wept at that testimony.[4]

As both the *Seattle Times* and the *Star* demonstrated throughout the summer and autumn of 1906, the boundary dividing "facts" and "values" can easily blur. Both newspapers' circulation efforts nurtured a tendency to invoke dearly held values (such as family, responsibility, loyalty) and heartrending images as a way to create drama. This combined with the maudlin writing style of those newspapers to make George Mitchell a hero and to obscure the fact that he had stalked a man and killed him in cold blood. In the spinning of dramatic tales, some of the critical facts dropped out.

Dramatic writing aside, the story itself was a natural magnet for all kinds of reportorial embroidery. Indeed, it would have been exceedingly difficult for the press to capture the significance and human drama of Mitchell's murder of Edmund Creffield without noting the broader issues of family and responsibility. That is, of course, precisely the point. In explaining the twists and turns of the Creffield saga, the press invariably alluded to larger issues, to a broad constellation of values cherished by so many, that made this case so compelling. But the result was an unbalanced indictment of Creffield and a romanticizing of George Mitchell.

At times, the broader "values" simply overrode the facts. The canonization of George Mitchell by the Seattle afternoon newspapers depended in large part on the understanding that he had saved his "ruined" sisters. Consequently, Esther's insistence that she had never been seduced by Creffield received almost no attention. The sources most useful for advancing the broader story of family, loyalty, and duty were almost all opponents of Creffield. Even when contrarian voices—such as those of the Seattle prosecutors—were available, reporters paid them no heed. In that environment, the exact details were often lost, particularly if they undermined the larger lesson.

Press coverage of the Mitchell-Creffield case sometimes revealed more about the reporters' and editors' views than about the events themselves. The all-male reporting corps clearly admired the "manly" George Mitchell, and the journalists repeatedly let their own views color their stories. Creffield was no saint, to be sure, but nowhere was there any effort to describe—much less understand—the spiritual and anti-materialistic ideas that propelled him and his followers. Nowhere was there a sobering article about the dangers of vigilantism—until, of course, the vigilantism led to ever greater violence.

In the introduction to this book, I observed that my first exposure to news articles about George Mitchell's trial had particularly intrigued me because they seemed to be so much more than just a report about a courtroom event. The press, it is clear, went well beyond offering a mere report of the "facts" of the case; it also selected a distinct interpretive framework that invoked a wide array of traditional social values and beliefs. To some degree, this should be no surprise, given that the selection, presentation, and explanation of "facts" cannot exist in a value-free environment. Still, the press's remarkably active participation in this saga—its clear effect on the chain of events—was made possible largely by the newspapers' use of traditional values to explain and define the "facts." In following this tack, the press adopted a strong position in the cultural wars of that era, defending a way of life that could only be justified when it was heavily romanticized. And it wove all of this into the news of the day, turning that news into a morality play that transcended the boundaries of a regional scandal.

Notes

Introduction

1. Lee, *Daily Newspaper*, 718–19, 725–26.
2. Charles A. Dana, "Power of the Press," *St. Louis Republic*, July 25, 1888, 1.
3. Frederic R. Marvin, "Editors and Newspapers: A Sermon," (Portland, OR: George H. Hines, 1883), n.p.
4. W. I. Thomas, "The Psychology of Yellow Journalism," *American Magazine* 65 (March 1908), 495–96; Editorial, "Newspapers' Sensations and Suggestions," *The Independent* 62 (February 21, 1907), 450–51.
5. Lee, *Daily Newspaper*, 731.
6. Mencken, *Newspaper Days*, 262–63; *Newspaper Maker*, October 17, 1895, 4; July 28, 1897, 5; September 2, 1897, 8; *Woodburn (OR) Journalist*, August 14, 1897, 134; Smythe, "The Reporter," 306; Smythe, *Gilded Age Press*, 165; Dicken-Garcia, *Journalistic Standards*, 155–222.
7. Boswell and McConaghy, *Raise Hell*, 107; E. W. Scripps to George H. Scripps, January 18, 1888, subseries 1.2, box 26, folder 3, Scripps Corr.
8. Quoted in Bell and Offen, *Women, the Family, and Freedom*, 138; Harland, *Happy Home*, 69.
9. Wilson, *Woman in Transition*, 41, 110–14; Kraditor, *Ideas of the Woman Suffrage Movement*, 43–56, 68–74; Matthews, *Rise of the New Woman*, 3–35.
10. Matthews, 5; Henry Finck, "Are Womanly Women Doomed?" *The Independent* 53 (January 31, 1901), 269; Lyman Abbott, "Why Women Do Not Wish the Suffrage," *Atlantic Monthly* 92 (September 1903), 291.

1 Collision Course

1. This discussion of the history of Corvallis draws from Dicken and Dicken, *Making of Oregon*; Fagan, *History of Benton County*; Gaston, *Centennial History of Oregon*; Carey, *History of Oregon*; and Martin, "History of Corvallis."
2. *Corvallis Times*, June 27, 1903, 1.
3. Ibid., July 22, 1903, 2.
4. Ibid.; Reynolds, *Corvallis*, 13.
5. *Corvallis Times*, April 15, 1903, 3; Reynolds, *Corvallis*, 14–15.
6. *Corvallis Times*, April 1, 1903, 3; April 11, 1903, 3; May 9, 1903, 3; May

16, 1903, 3; May 27, 1903, 3; June 27, 1903, 3; June 30, 1903, 3; *Corvallis Gazette,* July 29, 1904, 5; August 25, 1904, 3; December 29, 1905, 3; December 22, 1905, 3.

7. *Corvallis Times,* June 27, 1903, 1.

8. This discussion of Creffield is drawn from the Portland *Oregon Journal,* August 1, 1904, 1; McDonald, *Roll, Ye Sinners,* 5; McKinley, *Marching to Glory,* 81; and *Corvallis Times,* August 6, 1904, 3.

9. Taiz, *Hallelujah,* 59–63.

10. History of the Salvation Army in Oregon, Salvation Army Web site (http://www.tsacascade.org); Hattersley, *Blood and Fire,* 155.

11. Despite the opposition it faced, the Salvation Army began to acquire an image of respectability in the United States by the late 1890s and early 1900s, as it reduced the emotionalism of its meetings and placed greater emphasis on its social-welfare programs. Taiz, *Hallelujah,* 156–57; "The Salvation Army in the United States, Christmas, 1899," in Booth-Tucker, *Salvation Army,* n.p.

12. *Seattle Times,* July 2, 1906, 1.

13. McCracken and Blodgett, *Holy Rollers,* 16–17, 19–22; McDonald, *Roll, Ye Sinners,* 10.

14. Reynolds, *Corvallis,* 51–52.

15. McDonald, *Roll, Ye Sinners,* 21–23.

16. Ibid.

17. Reynolds, *Corvallis,* 51.

18. *Corvallis Times,* June 10, 1903, 3.

19. Ibid.

20. Anderson, *Vision of the Disinherited,* 45; Synan, *Holiness-Pentecostal Movement,* 91.

21. The following account comes from the *Corvallis Times,* October 31, 1903, 2; November 4, 1903, 3; and the *Portland Oregonian,* November 3, 1903, 4.

2 The Shame of Corvallis

1. *Corvallis Gazette,* November 10, 1903, 3, 2; *Corvallis Times,* November 4, 1903, 2.

2. *Corvallis Gazette,* April 26, 1904, 1; August 23, 1904, 3; October 4, 1904, 2; February 23, 1906, 2; May 4, 1906, 3; May 11, 1906, 2; *Corvallis Times,* March 25, 1903, 3.

3. *Corvallis Gazette,* July 13, 1906, 2; *Corvallis Times,* July 15, 1903, 2; May 13, 1903, 3; December 13, 1904, 3; February 19, 1900, 3; August 27, 1902, 3.

4. *N.W. Ayer & Son's American Newspaper Annual,* Philadelphia: N.W. Ayer & Son, 1903, 718; Ibid., 1904, 715. For a broader discussion of political jour-

nalism in the United States, see Baldasty, *Commercialization of News*; and Smith, *Press, Politics and Patronage.*

5. *Corvallis Gazette*, August 26, 1904, 1; February 5, 1904, 5; *Corvallis Times*, April 11, 1903, 2; July 22, 1903, 2; *Corvallis Gazette*, December 8, 1905, 2; *Corvallis Times*, April 11, 1903, 2; *Corvallis Gazette*, July 13, 1906, 2; *Corvallis Times*, July 15, 1903, 2; May 13, 1903, 3; December 13, 1904, 3; February 19, 1900, 3; *Corvallis Times*, May 13, 1903, 3; August 27, 1902, 3.

6. *Corvallis Gazette*, February 19, 1900, 3; November 15, 1904, 3; *Corvallis Times*, August 27, 1902, 3; December 17, 1902, 3; December 31, 1902, 2; January 3, 1903, 4; December 13, 1902, 3; April 1, 1903, 2; April 11, 1903, 2; May 23, 1903, 2; *Corvallis Gazette*, November 3, 1903, 2; February 5, 1904, 5; *Corvallis Times*, January 7, 1903, 2, 4.

7. *Corvallis Times*, October 10, 1903, 2.

8. Ibid., May 2, 1903, 3.

9. Ibid., September 28, 1901, 3; September 10, 1902, 2; April 1, 1903, 3; January 7, 1903, 4; September 10, 1902, 2; June 7, 1903, 3; *Corvallis Gazette*, October 24, 1905, 3; September 22, 1905, 4.

10. *Corvallis Times*, April 24, 1901, 2; March 18, 1903, 3; April 29, 1903, 4; *Corvallis Gazette*, December 8, 1905, 2.

11. *Corvallis Gazette*, September 25, 1905, 2; *Corvallis Times*, January 7, 1903, 2.

12. *Corvallis Times*, May 13, 1903, 3.

13. Ibid., June 27, 1903, 1.

14. *Corvallis Gazette*, November 11, 1904, 1; *Corvallis Times*, June 27, 1903, 2, 3.

15. *Corvallis Times*, June 24, 1903, 3; June 27, 1903, 3; October 11, 1902, 2.

16. Ibid., April 7, 1903, 2.

17. Ibid., May 13, 1903, 2.

18. Ibid., October 31, 1903, 2.

19. Ibid.

20. Ibid.

21. Ibid., November 4, 1903, 3.

22. Ibid.

23. Ibid.

24. Ibid., November 7, 1903, 3; *Corvallis Gazette*, November 10, 1903, 3.

25. *Corvallis Gazette*, November 25, 1903, 3; *Corvallis Times*, November 24, 1903, 3.

26. *Corvallis Times*, January 6, 1904, 2.

27. Ibid.

28. Ibid.

29. Ibid.

30. Ibid., January 9, 1904, 2.

31. Ibid.

32. *Corvallis Gazette,* January 12, 1904, 2.

33. *Portland Oregonian,* January 8, 1904, 4; *Salem Statesman,* January 9, 1904, 2.

34. *Portland Oregonian,* February 1, 1904, 3; *Corvallis Times,* February 3, 1904, 4.

35. *Corvallis Times,* January 9, 1904, 2.

3 Weak Women

1. Wood-Allen, *Ideal Married Life,* 57; Horton, *Art of Living Together,* 79; Moore, *Social Ethics and Society Duties,* 63.

2. Parkhurst, *Talks to Young Women,* 10, 25, 27.

3. Havelock Ellis, "The Mental Differences of Men and Women," *The Independent* 58 (February 23, 1905), 412; Mitchinson, *Nature of Their Bodies,* 36, 280–82, 299; Haller. and Haller, *Physician and Sexuality,* 50–59; Hammond, "Nerves and the American Woman"; Ehrenreich and English, *Complaints and Disorders,* 25.

4. Mitchinson, *Nature of Their Bodies,* 58, 81; Morantz-Sanchez, *Conduct Unbecoming,* 120–21; Haller and Haller, *Physician and Sexuality,* 58–59; Wood-Allen, *Ideal Married Life,* 117; Rothman, *Woman's Proper Place,* 24–25. Also see Vertinsky, *Eternally Wounded Woman.*

5. *Corvallis Gazette,* December 19, 1905, 1.

6. *Corvallis Times,* April 15, 1903, 3.

7. *Corvallis Gazette,* December 15, 1905, 3; *Corvallis Times,* May 23, 1903, 3; June 7, 1903, 3; *Corvallis Gazette,* October 30, 1903, 2; *Corvallis Times,* June 27, 1903, 3; July 25, 1903, 3; *Corvallis Gazette,* April 13, 1906, 3.

8. *Corvallis Gazette,* May 3, 1904, 3.

9. *Corvallis Times,* November 4, 1903, 4, 3; January 9, 1904, 2.

10. *Corvallis Gazette,* January 12, 1904, 2.

11. Esther entered the home on November 18, 1903 (*Seattle Post-Intelligencer,* July 6, 1906, 2).

12. Ibid.

13. Ibid.

14. Ibid.; *Oregon Journal,* July 29, 1904, 1.

15. *Corvallis Times,* March 23, 1904, 3.

16. *Corvallis Gazette,* May 3, 1904, 3; *Portland Oregonian,* July 30, 1904, 5.

17. *Seattle Star,* July 3, 1906, 1.

18. *Corvallis Gazette,* May 3, 1904, 3; June 24, 1904, 4.

19. Ibid., May 3, 1904, 3.

20. *Seattle Star,* July 3, 1906, 1.

21. *Corvallis Gazette,* May 10, 1904, 3; June 14, 1904, 1.

22. Gamwell and Tomes, *Madness in America,* 164–65.

23. The story of Creffield's capture comes from the *Corvallis Times*, August 3, 1904, 3; July 30, 1904, 3; August 6, 1904, 2.

24. Ibid., July 30, 1904, 3; August 3, 1904, 3.

25. *Oregon Journal*, August 4, 1904, 3.

26. *Oregon Journal*, September 16, 1904, 1.

27. *Corvallis Times*, September 3, 1904, 2; August 6, 1904, 2.

28. The Portland trial account here and following comes from the *Oregon Journal*, September 16, 1904, 1.

29. *Corvallis Times*, September 21, 1904, 2.

30. *Corvallis Gazette*, September 20, 1904, 3.

31. Ibid., October 4, 1904, 3; *Corvallis Times*, September 21, 1904, 3.

32. *Corvallis Gazette*, September 20, 1904, 3; December 15, 1905, 2.

33. Ibid., March 24, 1906, 5.

34. *Portland Oregonian*, July 4, 1906, 1.

35. Phillips and Gartner, *Murdering Holiness*, 96.

36. Ibid.; *Seattle Times*, July 2, 1906, 1.

37. *Corvallis Gazette*, April 27, 1906, 2.

38. *Corvallis Times*, July 10, 1906, 1.

39. *Seattle Times*, July 5, 1906, 1.

40. *Seattle Star*, July 4, 1906, 1.

41. *Portland Oregonian*, May 8, 1906, 1.

42. Ibid., May 3, 1906, 8.

4 The Press Proclaims a Hero

1. *Seattle Star*, May 7, 1906, 1, 3; *Seattle Times*, May 7, 1906, 1.

2. *Seattle Post-Intelligencer*, May 11, 1906, 5.

3. Carey, *Media, Myths, and Narratives*, 18; S. Elizabeth Bird and Robert W. Dardenne, "Myth, Chronicle and Story: Exploring the Narrative Qualities of News," in Carey, *Media, Myths, and Narratives*, 67, 71; Gregg Barak, "Media, Society and Criminology," in Barak, *Media, Process, and Crime*, 32.

4. *Newspaperdom*, July 1892, 3.

5. *Pittsburgh Leader*, January 21, 1898, 8.

6. *Newspaper Maker*, May 14, 1896, 4.

7. *Seattle Times*, May 6, 1906, Magazine section, 3.

8. Ibid., May 5, 1906, 1; May 2, 1906, 1.

9. Ibid., May 4, 1906, 6.

10. Boswell and McConaghy, *Raise Hell*, 138.

11. *Seattle Times*, May 3, 1906, 1.

12. Ibid., May 4, 1906, 1.

13. Ibid.

14. E. H. Wells to E. W. Scripps, February 1, 1906, subseries 1.1, box 26, folder 6, Scripps Corr.

15. Scripps to W. D. Wasson, January 23, 1904, subseries 1.2, box 5, folder 3, Scripps Corr.

16. Scripps to B. F. Gurley, September 6, 1906, subseries 1.2, box 7, folder 10; Scripps to W. D. Wasson, September 25, 1905, subseries 1.2, box 6, folder 3; Scripps to R. F. Paine, February 28, 1906, subseries 1.2, box 6, folder 17; Scripps to Paine, February 26, 1906, subseries 1.2, box 6, folder 17; Paine to Scripps, September 13, 1905, subseries 1.2, box 24, folder 7 (all Scripps Corr.).

17. *Seattle Star,* February 23, 1906, 1; February 9, 1906, 1; February 15, 1906, 1; February 22, 1906, 1; May 3, 1906, 1; May 5, 1906, 1.

18. *Seattle Times,* May 8, 1906, 1.

19. Ibid.

20. *Corvallis Gazette,* May 8, 1906, 1.

21. Ibid., June 26, 1906, 1. Emphasis added.

22. *Portland Oregonian,* May 9, 1906, 6; May 8, 1906, 1, 6; Portland *Oregon Journal,* May 8, 1906, 1.

23. *Portland Oregonian,* May 10, 1906, 6.

24. *Seattle Star,* May 11, 1906, 1.

25. Ibid., May 12, 1906, 1.

26. *Seattle Times,* May 15, 1906, 1.

27. *Seattle Times,* June 1, 1906, 1.

28. Bederman, *Manliness and Civilization,* 180; Rafford S. Pike, "What Men Like in Women," *Cosmopolitan* 31 (1900), 609–13 (quoted in Rotundo, *American Manhood,* 106).

29. Bederman, *Manliness and Civilization,* 180–81; Pieter Spierenburg, "Masculinity, Violence and Honor," in Spierenburg, *Men and Violence,* 2, 5.

30. Rotundo, *American Manhood,* 94.

31. McGovern, *Golden Censer,* 60.

32. *Corvallis Times,* May 8, 1906, 4.

33. *Seattle Star,* April 9, 1906, 4; April 21, 1906, 6.

34. Ibid., May 1, 1906, 7; May 5, 1906, 7.

35. *Seattle Times,* May 1, 1906, 9; May 2, 1906, 10; May 3, 1906, 11.

36. Stevens, *Sensationalism,* 42–53.

37. *Seattle Star,* May 7, 1906, 1, 3; May 9, 1906, 1; May 19, 1906, 1.

38. *Seattle Times,* May 8, 1906, 1; May 13, 1906, 1; June 1, 1906, 2; June 19, 1906, 6.

39. Ibid., May 8, 1906, 1; May 13, 1906, 1; May 11, 1906, 1; *Seattle Star,* May 19, 1906, 1.

40. *Seattle Star,* May 8, 1906, 1 (the *Star* describes the lone male as a rather lazy man who was married to one of Creffield's female devotees); *Seattle Times,* May 11, 1906, 1; *Seattle Star,* May 11, 1906, 1; May 8, 1906, 1; May 11, 1906, 1; May 18, 1906, 1.

41. *Seattle Times,* May 8, 1906, 1; *Seattle Star,* May 7, 1906, 3.

42. *Seattle Star*, May 11, 1906, 1.

43. *Seattle Times*, June 1, 1906, 2.

44. Ibid.

45. *Seattle Star*, May 7, 1906, 3.

46. *Seattle Times*, May 7, 8, 11, 13, 15, 16, 19, and June 1, 19, 24, 1906; *Seattle Star*, May 7, 8, 9, 10, 12, 15, 19, 1906.

47. *Seattle Times*, June 1, 1906, 1.

48. Ibid., May 11, 1906, 1.

49. *Seattle Star*, May 12, 1906, 1; May 11, 1906, 1; May 9, 1906, 1.

50. Ibid., June 1, 1906, 1.

51. *Seattle Times*, May 13, 1906, 1.

52. *Seattle Star*, May 9, 1906, 1.

53. *Seattle Argus*, May 12, 1906, 1.

54. Ibid.

55. Ibid.

56. *Seattle Star*, May 15, 1906, 7.

57. *Seattle Argus*, May 19, 1906, 1; *Corvallis Times*, June 22, 1906, 2; *Woodburn Independent*, May 17, 1906, 2; *Seattle Argus*, May 12, 1906, 1.

58. *Seattle Star*, May 15, 1906, 3.

59. Ibid., May 14, 1906, 6.

60. Ibid., May 19, 1906, 1.

5 Defending George Mitchell

1. Lessard, *Architect of Desire*.

2. *Seattle Star*, June 27, 1906, 1; June 25, 1906, 1; July 4, 1906, 1. Also see Mooney, *Evelyn Nesbit and Stanford White*.

3. *Seattle Times*, June 26, 1906, 1.

4. Hartog, "Lawyering," 67–97; *Seattle Times*, November 30, 1904, 12.

5. Herman, *Insanity Defense*, 5; Gerber, *Insanity Defense*, 24. Also see Biggs, *Guilty Mind*; Goldstein, *Insanity Defense*.

6. *Seattle Star*, June 26, 1906, 1; June 25, 1906, 1.

7. Ibid., June 26, 1906, 1.

8. Ibid., June 27, 1906, 1.

9. *Seattle Times*, June 27, 1906, 1.

10. Ibid.

11. *Seattle Star*, June 27, 1906, 1; *Seattle Times*, June 27, 1906, 1; June 28, 1906, 1.

12. *Seattle Times*, June 25, 1906, 1.

13. Ibid., June 28, 1906, 1.

14. Ibid., June 26, 1906, 1; June 25, 1906, 1.

15. Ibid., June 29, 1906, 2.

16. *Portland Oregonian*, June 30, 1906, 4.

17. Ibid.

18. *Seattle Times*, June 29, 1906, 2.

19. Ibid.; June 30, 1906, 2; *Seattle Star*, June 29, 1906, 1; *Seattle Times*, June 30, 1906, 2.

20. *Seattle Times*, June 28, 1906, 1.

21. Ibid., June 30, 1906, 2.

22. *Seattle Post-Intelligencer*, June 30, 1906, 2; *Portland Oregonian*, June 30, 1906, 2; *Seattle Times*, June 30, 1906, 2.

23. *Seattle Times*, July 1, 1906, 20; *Seattle Star*, June 30,1906, 1.

24. *Seattle Star*, June 30, 1906, 1; *Seattle Times*, July 1, 1906, 1, 20.

25. *Seattle Star*, July 2, 1906, 1.

26. Ibid., 11.

27. *Seattle Times*, July 1, 1906, 3.

28. *Seattle Star*, July 2, 1906, 1.

29. *Seattle Times*, July 2, 1906, 1.

30. Ibid.

31. *Seattle Star*, July 2, 1906, 1; *Seattle Times*, July 2, 1906, 1; *Seattle Post-Intelligencer*, July 2, 1906, 1; July 1, 1906, 7; *Seattle Times*, July 3, 1906, 1.

32. *Seattle Times*, July 1, 1906, 3; July 2, 1906, 1.

33. Ibid., July 1, 1906, 3.

34. Ibid., July 3, 1906, 1, 2; July 2, 1906, 1.

35. *Seattle Star*, July 3, 1906, 1.

36. *Seattle Times*, July 3, 1906, 1.

37. *Portland Oregonian*, July 3, 1906, 6; July 4, 1906, 1.

38. Ibid., July 4, 1906, 1, 5.

39. *Seattle Times*, July 2, 1906, 2; July 4, 1906, 1.

40. Ibid., July 4, 1906, 1.

41. Ibid., 2; *Seattle Post-Intelligencer*, July 6, 1906, 2.

42. *Seattle Times*, July 4, 1906, 1, 2.

43. Ibid, 1.

44. *Portland Oregonian*, July 8, 1906, 4; *Seattle Times*, July 7, 1906, 1.

45. *Seattle Post-Intelligencer*, July 6, 1906, 2.

46. *Seattle Star*, July 5, 1906, 1.

47. Ibid., July 6, 1906, 1.

48. *Corvallis Times*, July 10, 1906, 1; *Seattle Times*, July 5, 1906, 1; *Seattle Star*, July 5, 1906, 1.

49. *Seattle Star*, July 5, 1906, 1. Emphasis added.

50. Ibid.

51. Ibid., July 6, 1906, 1.

52. *Seattle Times*, July 7, 1906, 1; *Portland Oregonian*, July 8, 1906, 4.

53. *Seattle Times*, July 8, 1906, 1; *Seattle Star*, July 7, 1906, 1; *Seattle Times*, July 10, 1906, 1.

54. *Seattle Star*, July 10, 1906, 1.

55. Ibid.; *Seattle Times,* July 10, 1906, 1; *Seattle Post-Intelligencer,* July 11, 1906, 5.

56. *Seattle Post-Intelligencer,* July 11, 1906, 1; *Seattle Star,* July 11, 1906, 1; *Seattle Times,* July 11, 1906, 2.

57. *Portland Oregonian,* July 11, 1906, 1. Also see *Corvallis Times,* July 13, 1906, 1.

58. *Portland Oregonian,* July 11, 1906, 4.

59. *Corvallis Times,* July 13, 1906, 2.

6 Second Thoughts

1. *Seattle Star,* July 9, 1906, 1.
2. *Seattle Times,* July 8, 1906, 1.
3. Ibid., July 10, 1906, 1.
4. Ibid., 6.
5. Ibid., July 9, 1906, 3.
6. Ibid., July 11, 1906, 6. Steilacoom was the location of the state mental hospital, which still operates there as Western State Hospital.
7. Ibid., May 8, 1906, 1.
8. Ibid., July 11, 1906, 1.
9. Ibid.
10. *Woodburn Independent,* July 19, 1906, 1; *Seattle Post-Intelligencer,* July 17, 1906, 16.
11. *Seattle Argus,* July 14, 1906, 10.
12. *Seattle Star,* July 9, 1906, 1; July 11, 1906, 1.
13. *Seattle Post-Intelligencer,* July 13, 1906, 4.
14. Ibid.
15. Ibid.
16. *Seattle Star,* July 13, 1906, 4.
17. *Seattle Post-Intelligencer,* July 13, 1906, 4.
18. *Seattle Star,* July 13, 1906, 6.
19. *Seattle Times,* Extra Edition, July 12, 1906, 1; July 13, 1906, 1.
20. *Seattle Star,* July 6, 1906, 1; *Seattle Times,* July 13, 1906, 1.
21. *Seattle Times,* July 13, 1906, 2.
22. Ibid., 1.
23. *Seattle Star,* July 13, 1906, 1.
24. *Seattle Times,* July 13, 1906, 1.
25. *Seattle Star,* July 13, 1906, 4.
26. Ibid., 2; *Seattle Times,* July 13, 1906, 1.
27. *Seattle Star,* July 13, 1906, 1.
28. Ibid. July 17, 1906, 4; *Seattle Times,* July 17, 1906, 4; July 13, 1906, 3.
29. *Seattle Times,* July 13, 1906, 3.
30. Ibid.

31. Ibid.

32. *Seattle Star,* July 14, 1906, 1.

33. *Seattle Post-Intelligencer,* July 13, 1906, 3.

34. Ibid.

35. Ibid., 1.

36. *Corvallis Gazette,* July 16, 1906, 1; *Seattle Post-Intelligencer,* July 13, 1906, 1; *Corvallis Times,* July 13, 1906, 2.

37. *Seattle Post-Intelligencer,* July 13, 1906, 1.

38. *Seattle Star,* July 14, 1906, 1; July 13, 1906, 1, 7.

39. *Seattle Times,* July 16, 1906, 8; July 17, 1906, 8.

40. *Corvallis Times,* July 20, 1906, 1.

41. *Albany Weekly Herald,* July 19, 1906, 1; *Newberg Graphic,* July 19, 1906, 1.

7 Unforgiven

1. *Seattle Star,* July 23, 1906, 1.

2. Ibid., August 10, 11, 13, 14, 15, 16, 17, 18, 22, all p. 1; *Seattle Times,* August 1, 2, 4, 5, 9, 10, 11, 16, 17, 19, 22, 1906, all p. 1.

3. *Newberg Graphic,* July 19, 1906, 4.

4. *Seattle Post-Intelligencer,* July 18, 1906, 1. The statute provided that "Whenever any person shall be found by the superior court in any county to be insane, and such person has no legal residence within this state, such person shall be sent, at the expense of the state, to the place where such person belongs in every case where such place of residence can be ascertained. And it shall be the duty of the superior court at the time of the inquest to ascertain the place where such person belongs, when the same can be conveniently done. The sheriff of the county shall convey such person to the place where he belongs."

5. *Seattle Times,* July 13, 1906, 1; July 24, 1906, 5.

6. *Seattle Star,* July 14, 1906, 1.

7. *Seattle Times,* September 20, 1906, 1; September 21, 1906, 1.

8. *Seattle Star,* September 12, 1906, 7; September 14, 1906, 1; *Seattle Times,* September 21, 1906, 8.

9. *Seattle Post-Intelligencer,* September 19, 1906, 5.

10. *Seattle Post-Intelligencer,* September 21, 1906, 1.

11. *Seattle Times,* September 21, 1906, 1.

12. *Seattle Star,* September 21, 1906, 1.

13. *Seattle Times,* September 20, 1906, 1.

14. Ibid., September 21, 1906, 1.

15. Ibid., September 23, 1906, 1.

16. *State of Washington v. Superior Court for King County,* Brief of Respondents.

17. *State of Washington v. Superior Court for King County,* 258.

18. *State of Washington v. Superior Court for King County,* Brief of Respon-

dents on Constitutionality of Deportation Act, 4; *State of Washington v. Superior Court for King County*, Supplemental Brief of Petitioner, 12; *State of Washington v. Superior Court for King County*, Brief Submitted by the Attorney General, 4.

19. *Seattle Times*, November 17, 1906, 2.

20. *Corvallis Times*, November 20, 1906, 1.

21. Ibid., November 23, 1906, 1.

22. *Seattle Star*, November 20, 1906, 1.

23. *Seattle Times*, November 18, 1906, 1; November 17, 1906, 2; *Seattle Star*, November 20, 1906, 1.

24. *Seattle Times*, November 19, 1906, 2.

25. *State of Washington v. Superior Court for King County*, 251, 255.

26. Ibid., 258.

27. Western State Hospital for the Insane, Admissions; Western State Hospital for the Insane, Register of Discharges; *Yaquina Bay News* (Newport, OR), August 6, 1914, 1; *Corvallis Gazette*, August 7, 1914, 5.

8 News and Values

1. *Seattle Star*, May 19, 1906, 1.

2. *Seattle Times*, July 13, 1906, 1.

3. Ibid., June 25, 1906, 1; June 28, 1906, 1.

4. Ibid., July 4, 1906, 1.

Bibliography

Newspapers

Albany (OR) *Weekly Herald*
Corvallis *Gazette*
Corvallis *Times*
Newberg (OR) *Graphic*
Portland *Oregonian*
Portland *Oregon Journal*
Portland *Telegram*
Salem (OR) *Statesman*
Seattle *Argus*
Seattle Post-Intelligencer
Seattle *Star*
Seattle Times
Woodburn (OR) *Independent*

Manuscript Collection

E. W. Scripps Correspondence, Ohio University, Athens, Ohio (abbreviated as
   Scripps Corr. in notes)

Documents

*State of Washington, on the Relation of Kenneth Mackintosh, v. Superior Court for
   King County.* Case no. 6444, decided January 5, 1907. Washington Reports
   vol. 45. Seattle and San Francisco: Bancroft-Whitney, 1908.
*State of Washington, on the Relation of Kenneth Mackintosh, v. Superior Court for
   King County.* Brief of Respondents.
————. Brief of Respondents on Constitutionality of Deportation Act.
————. Brief Submitted by the Attorney General at the Request of the Above
   Mentioned Court.
————. Supplemental Brief of Petitioner.

Western State Hospital for the Insane. Admissions, Inmate Register 1871–
1915. Box 50, vol. 1, p. 64, Washington State Archives.
———. Register of Discharges, 1909. Box 68, np, Washington State Archives.

Books and Articles

Abramson, Phyllis L. *Sob Sister Journalism.* New York: Greenwood, 1990.

Adams, Oscar F. *The Presumption of Sex and Other Papers.* Boston: Lee and
Shepard, 1892.

Anderson, Robert M. *Vision of the Disinherited: The Making of American Pentecostalism.* New York: Oxford University Press, 1979.

Ayers, Edward L. *Vengeance and Justice: Crime and Punishment in the 19th Century
American South.* New York: Oxford University Press, 1984.

Baldasty, Gerald J. The *Commercialization of News in the Nineteenth Century.* Madison: University of Wisconsin Press, 1992.

Barak, Gregg, ed. *Media, Process, and the Social Construction of Crime: Studies in
Newsmaking Criminology.* New York: Garland, 1994.

Barth, Gunther. *City People: The Rise of Modern City Culture in Nineteenth-Century
America.* New York: Oxford University Press, 1980.

Bederman, Gail. *Manliness and Civilization: A Cultural History of Gender and Race
in the United States, 1880–1917.* Chicago: University of Chicago Press, 1995.

Bell, Susan G., and Karen M. Offen, eds. *Women, the Family, and Freedom: The
Debate in Documents.* Vol. 2, *1880–1950.* Stanford, CA: Stanford University
Press, 1983.

Beveridge, Albert J. *The Young Man and the World.* New York: D. Appleton, 1905.

Biggs, John Jr. *The Guilty Mind: Psychiatry and the Law of Homicide.* New York:
Harcourt Brace, 1955.

Blumhofer, Edith. *Restoring the Faith: The Assemblies of God, Pentecostalism, and
American Culture.* Urbana: University of Illinois Press, 1993.

Bolton, Sarah K. *Every-Day Living.* Boston: L.C. Page, 1900.

Booth-Tucker, Frederick. *The Salvation Army in America: Selected Reports, 1899–
1903.* New York: Arno , 1972.

Boswell, Sharon A., and Lorraine McConaghy. *Raise Hell and Sell Newspapers:
Alden J. Blethen and the Seattle Times.* Pullman: Washington State University
Press, 1996.

Camhi, Jane J. *Women Against Women: American Anti-Suffragism, 1880–1920.*
New York: Carlson, 1994.

Carey, Charles H. *History of Oregon.* Portland, OR: Pioneer Historical Publishing, 1922.

Carey, James W., ed. *Media, Myths, and Narratives: Television and the Press.* New-
bury Park, CA: Sage, 1988.

Cary, Ferdinand E. *The Standard Book of Knowledge, An American Home Educator,
Ten Great Books in One Volume.* N.p., 1904.

Chester, Elizabeth. *Girls and Women*. Boston: Houghton Mifflin, 1890.

———. *The Unmarried Woman*. New York: Dodd, Mead, 1892.

Connery, Thomas B. "Fusing Fictional Technique and Journalistic Fact: Literary Journalism in the 1890s Newspaper." PhD diss., Brown University, 1984.

Coppens, Charles. *Moral Principles and Medical Practice: The Basis of Medical Jurisprudence*. 2nd ed. New York: Benziger Brothers, 1897.

Deshon, George. *Guide for Catholic Young Women, Especially for Those Who Earn Their Own Living*. New York: Catholic Book Exchange, 1893.

Dicken, Samuel N., and Emily F. Dicken. *The Making of Oregon: A Study in Historical Geography*. Portland: Oregon Historical Society, 1979.

Dicken-Garcia, Hazel. *Journalistic Standards in Nineteenth-Century America*. Madison: University of Wisconsin Press, 1989.

Dodge, Grace H.. *A Bundle of Letters to Busy Girls on Practical Matters*. New York: Funk and Wagnalls, 1887.

Ehrenreich, Barbara, and Deirdre English. *Complaints and Disorders: The Sexual Politics of Sickness*. Old Westbury, NY: Feminist Press, 1973.

Fagan, David D. *History of Benton County, Oregon*. Portland, OR: A.G. Walling, 1885.

Flexner, Eleanor. *Century of Struggle: The Woman's Rights Movement in the United States*. New York: Atheneum, 1973.

Foote, Edward B. *Plain Home Talk About the Human System: The Habits of Men and Women, embracing medical common sense applied to causes, prevention, and cure of chronic diseases*. New York: Murray Hill, 1881.

Forster, Dora. *Sex Radicalism as Seen by an Emancipated Woman of the New Time*. Chicago: M. Harman, 1905.

Gamwell, Lynn, and Nancy Tomes. *Madness in America: Cultural and Medical Perceptions of Mental Illness Before 1914*. Ithaca, NY: Cornell University Press, 1995.

Gaston, Joseph. *The Centennial History of Oregon, 1811–1912*. Chicago: S.J. Clarke, 1912.

Gerber, Rudolph J. *The Insanity Defense*. Port Washington, NY: Associated Faculty Press, 1984.

Gilman, Nicholas P. *Conduct as Fine Art: The Laws of Daily Conduct*. Boston: Houghton Mifflin, 1892.

Glenn, Susan A. *Female Spectacle: The Theatrical Roots of Modern Feminism*. Cambridge, MA: Harvard University Press, 2000.

Goldstein, Abraham S. *The Insanity Defense*. New Haven, CT: Yale University Press, 1967.

Gosling, Francis G. *Before Freud: Neurasthenia and the American Medical Community, 1870–1910*. Urbana: University of Illinois Press, 1987.

Grob, Gerald N. *The Mad Among Us: A History of the Care of America's Mentally Ill*. New York: Free Press, 1994.

————.*Mental Illness and American Society, 1875–1940.* Princeton, NJ: Princeton University Press, 1983.

Haller, John S. Jr. "Neurasthenia: The Medical Profession and the 'New Woman' of the Late Nineteenth Century." *New York State Journal of Medicine* (Feb. 15, 1971), 473–82.

Haller, John S. Jr., and Robin M. Haller, *The Physician and Sexuality in Victorian America.* Carbondale: Southern Illinois University Press, 1995.

Halttunen, Karen. *Confidence Men and Painted Women: A Study of Middle-Class Culture in America, 1830–1870.* New Haven, CT: Yale University Press, 1982.

Hammond, Graeme M. "Nerves and the American Woman," *Harper's Bazar* 40:7 (July 1906), 590–93.

Harland, Marion. *The Secret of a Happy Home.* New York: Christian Herald, 1896.

Hartog, Hendrik. "Lawyering, Husbands' Rights, and 'the Unwrittten Law' in Nineteenth-Century America." *Journal of American History* 84:1 (1997), 67–97.

————. *Man and Wife in America: A History.* Cambridge, MA: Harvard University Press, 2000.

Hattersley, Roy. *Blood and Fire: William and Catherine Booth and Their Salvation Army.* New York: Doubleday, 2000.

Hermann, Donald H. J. *The Insanity Defense: Philosophical, Historical and Legal Perspectives.* Springfield, IL: Charles Thomas, 1983.

Hopkins, Ellice. *The Power of Motherhood, or Mothers and Sons: A Book for Parents and Those in Loco Parentis.* New York: E. P. Dutton, 1899.

Horton, Robert F. *On the Art of Living Together.* New York: Dodd, Mead, 1896.

Jordan, David S. *Life's Enthusiasms.* Boston: American Unitarian Association, 1906.

Kasson, John F. *Rudeness and Civility: Manners in Nineteenth-Century Urban America.* New York: Hill and Wang, 1990.

Kellogg, J. H. *Plain Facts for Old and Young: Embracing the Natural History of Hygiene of Organic Life.* Burlington, IA: I. F. Segner, 1891.

Knight, Graham, and Tony Dean. "Myth and the Structure of News." *Journal of Communication* 32:2 (1982), 144–57.

Kraditor, Aileen S. *The Ideas of the Woman Suffrage Movement, 1890–1920.* New York: Columbia University Press, 1967.

————. "Ideology of the Suffrage Movement." In Barbara Welter, ed., *The Woman Question in American History.* Hinsdale, IL: Dryden, 1973.

Kraditor, Aileen S., ed. *Up from the Pedestal: Selected Writings in the History of American Feminism.* Chicago: Quadrangle, 1968.

Lecky, William. *The Map of Life: Conduct and Character.* New York: Longmans, Green, 1899.

Lee, Alfred M. *The Daily Newspaper in America: The Evolution of a Social Instrument.* New York: Macmillan, 1937.

Lessard, Suzannah. *The Architect of Desire: Beauty and Danger in the Stanford White Family.* New York: Dial, 1996.

Maeder, Thomas. *Crime and Madness: The Origins and Evolution of the Insanity Defense.* New York: Harper and Row, 1985.

Martin, Bruce. "History of Corvallis, 1846–1900." Master's thesis, University of Oregon, 1938.

Marvin, Frederic R. *Consecrated Womanhood: A Sermon Preached in the First Congregational Church, Portland, Oregon.* New York: J. O. Wright, 1903.

Marzolf, Marion T. *Civilizing Voices: American Press Criticism, 1880–1950.* New York: Longman, 1991.

Matthews, Jean V. *The Rise of the New Woman: The Women's Movement in America, 1875–1930.* Chicago: Ivan R. Dee, 2003.

McCracken, T., and Robert B. Blodgett. *Holy Rollers: Murder and Madness in Oregon's Love Cult.* Caldwell, ID: Caxton, 2002.

McDonald, Marlene. *Roll, Ye Sinners, Roll: The Story of the Creffield Cult.* Philomath, OR: Benton County Historical Museum, privately printed, 2002.

McGovern, John. *The Golden Censer or the Duties of Today and the Hopes of the Future.* Chicago: Union Publishing House, 1882.

McKinley, Edward H. *Marching to Glory: The History of the Salvation Army in the United States, 1880–1992.* 2nd ed. Grand Rapids, MI: Eerdmans, 1995.

Mencken, H. L. *Newspaper Days, 1899–1906.* New York: Alfred A Knopf, 1941.

Mitchinson, Wendy. *The Nature of Their Bodies: Women and Their Doctors in Victorian Canada.* Toronto: University of Toronto Press, 1991.

Mooney, Michael M. *Evelyn Nesbit and Stanford White: Love and Death in the Gilded Age.* New York: William Morrow, 1976.

Moore, Mrs. Bloomfield H. *Social Ethics and Society Duties Through Education of Girls for Wives and Mothers and for Professions.* Boston: Estes and Lauriat, 1892.

Morantz-Sanchez, Regina. *Conduct Unbecoming a Woman: Medicine on Trial in Turn-of-the-Century Brooklyn.* New York: Oxford University Press, 1999.

Parkhurst, Charles H. *Talks to Young Women.* New York: Century, 1897.

Peiss, Kathy. "'Charity Girls' and City Pleasures: Historical Notes on Working-Class Sexuality, 1880–1920." In Jennifer Scanlon, ed., *The Gender and Consumer Culture Reader.* New York: New York University Press, 2000.

Phillips, Jim, and Rosemary Gartner. *Murdering Holiness: The Trials of Franz Creffield and George Mitchell.* Vancouver: University of British Columbia Press, 2003.

Probst, Otto E. *Secret Sins of Society and Philosophy of the Sexes Embracing the Interchangeable Relations of Man and Woman.* Chicago: American Publishing House, 1901.

Reynolds, Minerva Kiger. *Corvallis in 1900.* Philomath, OR: Benton County Historical Museum, n.d.

Rothman, Sheila. *Woman's Proper Place: A History of Changing Ideals and Practices, 1870 to the Present.* New York: Basic Books, 1978.

Rotundo, E. Anthony. *American Manhood: Transformation in Masculinity from the Revolution to the Modern Era.* New York: Basic Books, 1993.

Sangster, Margaret E. *The Art of Being Agreeable.* New York: Christian Herald, 1897.

Schlesinger, Arthur M. *Learning How to Behave: A Historical Study of American Etiquette Books.* New York: Macmillan, 1946.

Smith, Culver. *The Press, Politics and Patronage: The American Government's Use of Newspapers, 1789–1875.* Athens: University of Georgia Press, 1977.

Smith-Rosenberg, Carroll. *Disorderly Conduct: Visions of Gender in Victorian America.* New York: Alfred A. Knopf, 1985.

Smythe, Ted Curtis. *The Gilded Age Press, 1865–1900.* Westport, CT: Praeger, 2003.

———. "The Reporter, 1880–1900: Working Conditions and Their Influence on the News." *Journalism History* 7:1 (1980), 1–17.

Spierenburg, Pieter, ed. *Men and Violence: Gender, Honor, and Rituals in Modern Europe and America.* Columbus: Ohio State University Press, 1998.

Stage, Sarah. *Female Complaints: Lydia Pinkham and the Business of Women's Medicine.* New York: Norton, 1979.

Stevens, John D. *Sensationalism and the New York Press.* New York: Columbia University Press, 1991.

———. "Social Utility of Sensational News: Murder and Divorce in the 1920s." *Journalism Quarterly* 62:2 (Spring 1985), 53–58.

Surette, Ray, ed. *Justice and the Media.* Springfield, IL: Charles Thomas, 1984.

Synan, Vinson. *The Holiness-Pentecostal Movement in the United States.* Grand Rapids, MI: Eerdmans, 1971.

Taiz, Lillian. *Hallelujah Lads and Lasses: Remaking the Salvation Army in America, 1880–1930.* Chapel Hill: University of North Carolina Press, 2001.

Talmage, Thomas D. *Woman, Her Power and Privileges: A Series of Sermons on the Duties of the Maiden, Wife and Mother and of Their Influence in the Home and Society.* New York: J. S. Ogilvie, 1888.

Turnbull, George S. *History of Oregon Newspapers.* Portland: Binfords and Mort, 1939.

Vertinsky, Patricia. *The Eternally Wounded Woman: Women, Doctors and Exercise in the Late Nineteenth Century.* Manchester, U.K.: Manchester University Press, 1990.

Wilson, Margaret G. *The American Woman in Transition: The Urban Influence, 1870–1920.* Westport, CT: Greenwood, 1979.

Wood-Allen, Mary. *Ideal Married Life: A Book for All Husbands and Wives.* New York: Revell, 1901. Reprint, Farmingdale, NY: Dabor Social Science Publications, 1978.

Index

man interest and working-class issues, 77

Seattle Argus: attacks Mitchell, 92–93; attacks temporary insanity defense, 135–36

Seattle Post-Intelligencer: avoids sensationalism, 92, 147

Seattle Star, 77–78; attacks Esther Mitchell, 142, 144; attacks insanity hearings, 156; demonizes Creffield, 112; justifies murder of Creffield, 88, 144; Mitchell portrayed as hero in, 87–90; predicts acquittal for George Mitchell, 123–24; reinforces traditional gender roles for women, 84–85, 95–96

Seattle Times, 9, 74–76; attacks insanity hearings, 156–57; belated praise for prosecutors, 134–35; criticizes Esther Mitchell, 116, 141–42; defends Mitchell, 80, 117; demonizes Creffield, 86–87, 113; and Emory case, 131–33; invokes notion of "weak" women, 116; justifies murder of Creffield, 88; Mitchell portrayed as hero in, 87–90; predicts acquittal of Mitchell, 125; temporary insanity defense and, 132, 133; reinforces traditional gender roles for women, 85–86, 116

Shipley, Silas (defense attorney), 100, 113

Starr, Belle. *See* Mitchell, Donna

Starr, Burgess (Burt), 56, 119

temporary insanity defense, 102–3, 113–15, 125, 131–33, 136, 147, 153–58

Thaw, Evelyn Nesbit, 99

Thaw, Harry, 98–100

Thompson, Chester, 130–33

"unwritten law," 102

Wappenstein, Charles (Seattle police chief), 109, 139, 147

"weak women," 42, 50–52, 116; and commitment to asylums, 58–60

White, Stanford, 98–100

Whittlesey, Charlotte, 130

Wood-Allen, Dr. Mary, 50, 52